The Sohbat Ser

The Sohbat Series

This series captures the intensely personal journey of the spiritual wayfarer's path to wisdom and enlightenment. Encompassing everything from edifying lessons to powerful love poetry, these books explore the most intimate reflections and experiences of disciples at the hands of their spiritual masters.

Each volume is distinct in structure and form, mirroring the unique, extraordinary bond that exists between novice and sage. These personal recollections of both one-to-one and collective experiences will enable you, the reader, to savour the presence of the Shaykh who so enraptured the heart of the disciple.

Other books in the series:

The School of Celestial Fire: A Sufi Master Teaches
John Lindsay
(Shaykh Abdullah Sirr-Dan Al-Jamal)

~

The Merciful Door: Living with a Sufi Teacher in India
Scott Siraj al-Haqq Kugle
(Pir Rasheed Kaleemi)

Praise for the Book

Has a depth and love which makes me gasp… so honest and truthful with… an 'unworlded' beauty.

DEREK WEBSTER
An English poet

In our multicultural contemporary world, in which differences become more pregnant due to the online revolution and intensive transnational travel, Paul Sutherland's book is a breakthrough in the search for new, more relational paths of understanding cultural difference.

MONICA MANOLACHI
Romanian translator, essayist and poet

These pieces, poems and prose, impart a stirring impression of the encounter between the would-be novice and his master, as well as the environment in which it takes place. The writings are convincingly sincere, full of well-observed detail, psychological insight and a good bit of subtle humour. A very enjoyable read and a rare glimpse into the 'inner workings' of a seeker and the soul of a poet.

RUDHIA SHUKRULLAH
Translator, editor, and disciple of Shaykh Efendi

A journey evoking the sights, sounds and scents of Lefke, Cyprus, interwoven with spiritual seeking and the otherworldly holiness that surrounded a modern-day Sufi saint. Sutherland explores human vulnerability and spirituality, loss and grief in his verses, flirting with insanity, the curious, the mundane and the sacred amongst orange and olive tree groves, the crash of the ocean's surf, mosques and prayer rugs, and the scents of jasmine, dusty lanes and evergreens.

RABIA'S POETIC LICENCE

Servant of
the Loving One

First published in the UK by Beacon Books and Media Ltd
Earl Business Centre, Dowry Street, Oldham, OL8 2PF, UK.

www.beaconbooks.net

ISBN: 978-1-912356-63-8   Paperback
ISBN: 978-1-912356-64-5   Hardback
ISBN: 978-1-912356-65-2   eBook

Cover photograph and author photograph © Kazem Hakimi

Cataloging-in-Publication record for this book is available from the British Library

Servant of
the Loving One

Paul Abdul Wadud Sutherland

BEACON BOOKS

Contents

About the Author

Paul Sutherland, a British-Canadian poet and writer, arrived in the UK in 1973. He reverted to Islam in 2004 and became a follower of Shaykh Nazim al-Haqqani. He was given the name Abdul Wadud, servant of the Loving One. He went on Hajj in 2006, experiencing spiritual events and visions which confirmed the essential truth of Islam and the need all true seekers have for a distinguished guide. In Shaykh Nazim, former representative of religion at the UN, the poet had the best guide possible. Maulana Shaykh passed away in May 2014 but Paul (Abdul Wadud) Sutherland carries on with his Sufi practices—the prescribed daily prayers, giving alms, fasting during Ramadan, remembering Allah ﷻ and the Prophet Muhammad ﷺ through *dhikr*, reading of Qur'an and Sufi mystical books and through his own writing. He owes so much to his dear Shaykh who rescued him from his ego, vain desires of the world and put the *murid* on the path towards peace, enlightenment and love towards creation. May Allah ﷻ bless the soul of Shaykh Nazim al-Haqqani—a wonder of humanity and one of Allah's ﷻ great gifts to the people of the Earth. May we all learn respect for our fellow human beings and creation for the benefit of us all. Paul Abdul Wadud's love for his Shaykh has led to much poetry and fiction in which the poet has attempted to express the conditions of holiness he observed in and experienced from his beloved Maulana.

PART ONE

A Sufi Novice in Shaykh Efendi's Realm

DAYS WITHOUT LIGHT

Twisting island lanes
the whole night blacked-out
all the stars betrayed
a dead wife's face.

I stood in grey groves
by a small stone boat, flooded
with pink red carnations—
my beloved's grave.

All the quiet morning,
each mourner who came by
stuck in another flower stem
hoping it wouldn't wilt.

At midday rain seeped
her red earth at last moistened
our praying voices went on
with distancing crows.

Twilight still cloaked
under hollowed street lamps.
I strolled home, along verges
as if crossing a bridge.

Crude high beams passing
I too had died, sleep-walking
the land, guessing what
the angel might ask.

THE MOSQUE ATTENDANT

The new convert, Abdul Wadud, hadn't been in the Shaykh's realm many days when he met a stout and what seemed an unpredictable man. Vigorously, he shook AW's hand over a mosque's low boundary wall. They exchanged greetings—Abdul Wadud in confused Arabic, the other with some picked-up English words. He knew AW was English and from his pocket, without hesitation, took out a many times folded, square piece of lined paper, and handed it to the visitor. Curious, AW opened it like a strange flat flower and guessed a hint of perfume. After absorbing the handwritten words, he glanced up at the man again and this time saw beyond the mosque's grounds, with its minaret just taller than the whitish green leaves hanging from a date palm.

Earlier, on the valley's sparser side, Abdul Wadud had climbed a knoll and ducked down under a half-blocked archway, almost crawling into the cavity of a small abandoned church. Above the entrance, a Maltese cross was half-erased. Inside, the plaster in places had flaked off, exposing an under-pattern with mountain stream rocks: the building materials once used to construct this sacred shelter. It had been left to tumble down, with heaps of rubble disfiguring its perhaps beautiful tiled floor, the roof just intact.

The mosque attendant wore simple clothes in reserved colours, much more modest than the climbers in the hotel courtyard where earlier AW had a Turkish coffee. Abdul Wadud again read the words on the unfolded paper as if he had difficulty taking in the meaning or was hedging for time. English words that had been inscribed twice: one script far more elegant than the other, a date crossed out. AW questioned for a moment who had written the fine words for him. The first chaotic near illegible attempt perhaps his own; the second penned with precision and balance—a calligrapher, maybe—as a special present for the man in Abdul Wadud's language: *I lost my wife and children in an earthquake three years ago.* The first words mirrored the second; there was no doubt about their message. AW looked at the other man, unable to ask anything or expect a response to expand on the one line statement. He saw the emotion printed on his communicant's face that yet was veiled. AW returned the precious paper, refolding it, noticing the words' gradual disintegration. He thought, first the event, then the memory, then the record of the event; each in turn in ruins.

Then the mosque attendant leaned forward, pointing the tip of his forefinger against AW's chest. Abdul Wadud suspected he desired money; needed it not having a family, needed for a token of AW's empathy. The strong, sun-browned man would've taken language. In its absence he accepted £5. Before AW closed his wallet, the recipient produced from his left trouser pocket: one euro, 10 cents, two dollars and a necklace of uncertain value.

The novice understood the man wanted to give something for his £5. AW chose the shiny chain and tried to fasten it around his neck. The chain's circle and catch were too fine for his fingers. He gestured he would need help, half-turning to expose his nape. He leaned backwards against the mosque's low wall. The attendant drew aside AW's hair. His big, tough hands closed the necklace's link with ease, as if he'd done the same for his now deceased wife many times.

MIDDLE OF THE NIGHT

In seclusion AW in the past would have, sooner or later, started chattering to himself aloud with increased vigour. He'd march around shouting at the walls, the conclusions of some fierce argument with someone. He always knew who, but opponents often changed in the onslaught. He liked to think that great poetry came from arm-thrashing self-debate and wild linking of ideas. After, sometimes for hours, he'd dive into depression, exhausted from the effort and often his throat hoarse from his series of bombasts. Finally he'd fear he'd never cease: the debate an endless rant, then he would go quiet abruptly like a child halts howling and no one understands why. That night, he didn't fight the candle or the elongated shadows on the plaster. He counted many *salawāt,* over and over, praising the Prophet ﷺ. That repetition calmed the wordy rage wanting to break out. No one knew about AW's self-bent volubility. But AW pictured the Shaykh's pupils penetrating right into his craziest place. With the master, he had to space out his encounters, bow his head, shy from exact eye exchanges. Yet the sonorous tone of the word 'Maulana' comforted. His ears blushed from that ancient legendary sound—not too hard, kind and gentle, teasing and limpid—from its poised three syllable resonance and romance: earth, heaven and the unknown.

He believed Maulana's heart could expand and hold him in this lit corner, out-encompass darkness; be a further loop, a mountain necklace, that a dreamer strolled through unharmed, a band to contain and set a boundary to any unenlightened abyss. The Shaykh's small, old human heart's great out-reach could touch God's in-reach: oceanic waves of love drowning the earth. More than a brushing glance, AW guessed, intermingled with the Infinite's breath—a joint trumpet crying toward us.

IN NORTH CYPRUS; LEFKE
IN A YELLOW FIELD; ON A GREEN ISLE

To Maulana, my Sufi Shaykh, nearly 90

Night's soundless *tasbīhs*...
the Northern Star will guide some
but your heart's my compass

your tagged eyes can't hide
your Spring insights, weakling hands
your fate-bending love

your recurrent cough
can't obscure your balmy breath
or its truth-telling.

My small grandchild says
'yellow'—giving up on books
in lemony fields

her mum pressing green
between both hands' forefingers
blows an eagle screel

if we climb too high
too far, border guards might shoot...
intending to miss.

Tallest Troodos in view
on the window sill
black ants go berserk

where the path levels
a chair just like Van Gogh's sits
in a yellow haze

a donkey might speak
the mystery, a mustard bloom
might not be averse.

Old Lover must yield
to Beloved, no matter how long
he's worn the fragrance

your un-turbaned head's
too tender to be human
yet a gem-dotted orb

in your chair slumping,
Sayyidi, your words and thoughts rise
above Orion's belt.

Changing each second
East and West angles—Allah ﷻ is
the cosmic plumb line

the Lover accepts
the Beloved's unbreakingness
like night's high mirror

on a yellow bank
more than coincidence—there's
new views, new pleasures

still the Lover longs
to share his Lord's endless work
foretasting His Love

still *Sayyidi* you know
enlightening's possible
in each yellow field.

The child of no-time
forgets she's human and darts off
leap-frogging mountains.

'We must die' I hear
you say under-breath—asking
That One's forgiving

as if forgetting
when you quest my name—I say
'I'm your weakest servant.'

A cheering robin
lights on the ashen prong
of a sparse-leafed fig

alabaster Spring snow
on Olympus—forecasts
the *wadi*'s gushing

two little birds dance
round gloves of prickly pear
in twilit purple.

I kneel, make *sajda*
before the Lord of Creation
as day enters night

you, my Shaykh, might be
at rest and more awake than
anyone can wonder

and if your Lord hints...
you'll fly through the blackest place
to rescue a soul.

A CURE FOR HAY FEVER

On the warped board, a Cyprus grapefruit
you clutch in your hands, rub its cheeks

not yet wanting to taste this blessed
gift from the Shaykh, its tropical scent.

Deep or thin covered, your thumb
stroking its gold-yellow pitted skin,

you refuse to plunge inside. Let it
stay a rescued ornament, moon-

bright: surface cratered, a soft Scarface,
you imagine attacks it endured

in a walled, exile's garden, quaking
with others on the same ropey

branches. Hurricane-flailed, it kept
its outward crust, never fell and burst.

You idle, longing to know: whose grip
brought it down before reaching yours?

AW'S DISEASE

His dear wife and other followers of Maulana had no problem in recognising AW despite his sickly appearance. But *Sayyidi*, that is the teacher, the Shaykh, hadn't acknowledged who AW was until he'd been recouping for a week, on the first of his sojourns in the Shaykh's realm. Surely, thought AW, Maulana knew who he was. But right in the middle of a talk the Holy Man had pointed at AW and asked in an alarmed voice, 'Who is that?' A chorus of *murids* echoed 'He's Sofina's husband, Abdul Wadud.' The Shaykh didn't answer with an assuring 'Oh yes' or 'OK' or in the special tone he used a few days later when the teacher would say 'Welcome' to AW. On the earlier occasion no 'You're welcome' came from the Shaykh's beard-encircled mouth. He simply went on with his talk or spiritual instruction, and without a word or gesture. This denial had sent AW to his sickbed and isolation. Sofina had chimed that he (AW) had become so dirty that the Shaykh couldn't see who he was, which reminded AW of when his mother refused to recognise him because he came in from vigorous boyhood play covered in mud. He knew he fantasised but he liked the story. His mum, he instantly recovered, would never disown him due to dirt. But the dirt Sofina referred to was not earth. She meant that AW had been contaminated by worldly interests and the Shaykh wouldn't welcome him until some of that grot was removed through a good dose of illness.

A WINTER WALK FROM LEFKE, THROUGH THE VALLEY, UP INTO THE HILLS, DOWN TO THE SEA AND BACK

Between V-ed red ruts
in yesterday's tractor-prints
an unsquashed grapefruit:

rusting coat of arms:
beyond elegant iron gate
a dew-swallowed grove

the white hill flickers
from burnt almond shrub
against unreachable blue

far mountain gullies
sparkle in the morning rays,
hide in mauve shadow

gold-black tiger birds
flit across the winding road
to the Mediterranean

walking its chanting shore
I'm tempted to skip
a million stones

submerged—with each swell—
flat, sun-smoothed boulders tremble
like basking creatures.

Touching with kind slaps
the sea, like our Shaykh, teases
then hurls a salt blob.

Up the coast, off
the road, in a grove where the fruit
shouldn't be eaten

I settle down for
midday prayer shaded by
a grave-digger's tent

his labour's end marked
by sandstone whitewashed couches
on all but one side

martyred youth,
saintly granny, a stillborn child,
stream through consciousness

when I open my eyes
over the boundary's broken wall—
the sea's aquamarine

the rains haven't yet come
I walk dusty verges back past
dense orange-specked rows

recollections follow,
plumes from carob wood fires
blue-grey olive slopes

feeble-limbed I return,
Lefke's rascals out of school
the sun below date fronds.

DAWN ADHÁN

White Jasmine and beryl Pakistani-Night-Plants
fragrance the expectant mosquito calm space.
From the open, bamboo-railed porch, toward
the soundless *wadi* (no light yet switched on)
last of night's fission shows Ursa major and
minor prancing round Draco's trailing stars.

A few dust-yard roosters crack a raca-raca-doo
raca-raca-doo as if taking in a sun ray's stray
smidgen, before our eyesight begins to detect
the first anxious ribbon on the eastern hill line.

Once observed, into the hardly altered blackness
a human voice, announces to creation the *adhān*,
faith in a Creator; pitch, tone rising, modulating
like sweet siren calls—there's no God but God—
then semi-darkness' hush resumes until crows lift
from gold date clusters with repeated caw-caws.

THE SHAYKH'S SEQUENCE

Not from sleep or drugs
from where comes this seeing gaze—
disciplining the heart?

In a big green door
look through a disused keyhole
a distant *mihrab*

at Pir Pasha's grave
black from so much devotion
long candle wax drips

at Witness's tomb
feel with so many *du'as*—
longest colour drips

Murida under
her 12th c. Plane tree—serves
almonds in date jam

drink rose water slow
under that Crusader tree—
almonds in date jam

every second day
she scrubs her forecourt, chasing
the Cypriot dust

someone's black shoes—
first day it's looked like rain—
by reservoir's puddle

stray white butterfly
under whitening clouds—first day
it's looked like rain

Bougainvillea,
Oleander, and this one—
a scent beyond name

blue Morning Glory,
Angel Trumpets, sniff this one—
a scent beyond name

late crescent moon
a remote companion star
above gold date palms

did I not see my Shaykh
walking between barking dogs
under gold date palms?

Listen to his stick
tapping the crumbling road edge
before a first sun beam?

Before Lefke's dawn
the big and little bear prance
around a dragon

strain neck muscles, watch
Ursa major and minor
dance round dim Draco.

Have I not smuggled
blessed tangerines and grapefruits
from my Shaykh's garden?

Not sleep-drug induced
from where comes his waking gaze—
his disciplined heart?

AW'S MISPLACED JACKET

At last the Imam, who had been ruffling through his pockets, produced the appropriate sized key to open the big green door. The locked Mosque offended AW but he let it pass. To whom was he going to complain? The well-shaved bald Imam was a little distrusting why AW sought a quick entry into his Mosque—well it was his, in a sense. Probably the conservative man conceded the rash man was a *murid* of the local saint, Shaykh Efendi, which explained everything. To make the operation a complete success required a further subterfuge—AW had to locate, secure and put his jacket on with speed, with 'did I do that?' that no one would notice, if there had been anyone beside the Imam and his one now too clingy adherent. Perhaps the Imam despaired AW might become his one follower, unshakeable as a loyal dog; this might explain the man's increasing aloofness which served AW to recover his outer garment without anyone's observation, that could have led to them thinking AW is a thief since who would be so nonsensical to leave their jacket in the Mosque, then pantingly return to snatch the thing like a bone. Or that at least AW took a liberty because whose jacket was it— the Imam's? AW may have been permitted to borrow it to keep warm but then expected to leave it in the Mosque, to carry on its interminable *dhikr*. But as it turned out AW ably lifted the coat off the white plastic chair without internal or external protest and quickly slipped his arms down the sleeves and placed the humble beast over his shoulders and around his waist. A masterful re-entry achieved. Remarkably the jacket was neither bitter about being abandoned in the first place nor irritated by being disturbed in the second—an exemplary Sufi. The Mosque deserved a long glance back, from which AW gleaned comfort that he had rescued his windcheater from the religious squabbling of thousands of years about what is right and what is wrong, without anyone apparently having the nous to realise the squabbling was probably in error—as his Shaykh had famously said, at least with legions of thought that swept through AW, 'You can be right and still be wrong.' A high station consideration. But equally there were exceptions.

THE VISITOR

At his impulsive arrival,
hunting for the lit path
to a Sufi master's house,
he stooped under curves
of an unopened jasmine.
A *wadi* sounded, running
to a calm roar, in its valley
mountain water searched
for its ocean and diverted
fed cloud-shaped orchards.
Sweet fragrance held him.
A hung moon altered steps
into apparitions on stone.
He rounded a bend to see
an old wall straying under
a lean-to roof; hurt, plaster
steps crept up to a wicker-
railed porch. Half-turning
he panned shadowless sky.

Assembled white iris, under
a date palm's serrated fonts,
spoke galaxies. A worn lamp
blued a breach in a doorway.

His greeting *as-salām alaykum*
carried away in midnight air
the visitor was called inside.

CYPRUS, NEW MORNING

Giant pink-orange
rising, stirs the orchard
with winter colours

white valley houses
catch. Somewhere lorries
growl at an ascent

warming beams
stripe the grove—a palm
waves its welcome.

THE BELOVED

I ask a scarecrow to speak, if it can, about
the Beloved ☙: it turns its straw head and says:

Beyond what pain is un-understandable
no further torture exists, not burning bars
but the Beloved's arms ready to welcome.
Be confused—who's beloved, who's you.
Can't separate; then accept, be bewildered:
a holy state, the blessedness that follows grief.
The Beloved is already approaching to hold
you between sense and nonsense. Be empty
as my straw legs and head, easily on fire.
Give up on reason, don't fantasise
you can outsmart the Eternal One
or keep your individual pursuits.
The Beloved will use you like a rag
to change the world you now despise.
What's beyond indiscernible sorrow, is Love.
Sniff it when you see the blank wall bloom
and try not to name it—rose or jasmine—
just say YOU over and over to the Beloved.

THE ADHÁN AT TWILIGHT IN TOWN

The Shaykh is the Pole, which everything hangs on. That thought almost silenced AW's speculations. Then the *adhān* sounded: modulating faith and its call to submission. A car interfered with a cough, another beeped its horn; a discordant dog howled joining in as best it could. But the climbing *Allah-hu-akbar*s swarmed through the air; ancient and full of songs of martyrs, those perfected in faith, voices of a billion faithful through earth, through history, mystics, scholars and builders, artists and pavement sweepers; declaring as once in Medina as once before battle, before love-making, before everything that the empty sky and shop is full, bursting with God's glory and presence, so great it can't and doesn't need to be seen.

Beautiful, subtle; making and un-doing, aware and delaying; healing and calling the living to death, calling them to wake and discover what's real and invaluable that time or drought can't deter. Now heard, more than the wind; a human voice like the wind, perhaps bringing rain, hope. Most pretended they didn't hear the clarion, as with the dawn *adhān* and slept through its call to rise from dreams and worship Allah ﷻ, honour His Messenger ﷺ. The *adhān* didn't change the direction of their feet, car journey or stop them eating kebab or drinking Turkish coffee and black tea. Citizens in the bank kept on with their dealing. What do they think when these words plunder the air, words in an idiom they know; big words that ravish space like invading harpies, but invisible and suddenly silent again; no police knocking on the door demanding an explanation for their unconcern. That something so powerful could fly past and leave it to our conscience, whether we engage or not, shocked AW. The power that needed nothing was what he believed in. The girl could go on sweeping in her doorway and not be punished, her hair not torn out or pitched; no car knocking her down on the way home. This was Allah ﷻ, the Loving One, whose voice mixed in the *adhān*. Think, thought AW, the petty shouts of generals, commanders, of troops or war helicopters or bank managers; those shouts don't go unheeded, people shake at such voices. But the greatest voice, the great call, the call of Allah ﷻ—everyone thinks they can ignore that.

31

A SEPTEMBER DAY OF RAIN

A few drops speckle
someone's old red baby chair—
thunder chuckling

what of Prophet's ﷺ flag?
Each tall reed waves its pennant
as rain starts to pit pat

it must be longed for
that the sandpaper mountains
will taste refreshment

the *dergāh* perfumed,
'there's only here and the planet'
Abdul Salaam says

raking out dead leaves
between iris—a distant
spring fragrance returns

a discreet shop-keeper
now releases skinny receipts
without my asking

a huge buzzing moth,
stunned by the candle's flicker,
creeps off the table

his arm in a cast
a youngster boasts—'I'm still good
at stoning crickets'

drips tingle off leaves
as heat comes back into the day,
the west brightening

two Aloe Veras
under the unused clothesline
do greenest *dhikr*

across the valley
young school-leaving voices,
an engine turns over

the *adhān* resounds
between my slow *salawāt:*
each pause mingling

sweet music of pines
draws Salih to a calm place:
I say they're 'soughing'

he's found shelter
'micro-waves can attack you—
stomach, heart or mind'

behind 20,000
of the Shaykh's *jinn* soldiers—he strolls
in plain inmate clothes

soon to be in the air
a grey beard *murid* asks me
to perform a *du'a*

a little lizard
follows mud wall crevices
like a hectic map

Ahmed-Omar's reached
the point where he can't stomach
another watermelon

the porch curtains hang
so slack—no breeze to chase off
a late summer fly

passing through my fingers
each bead opens a glimpse
on Muhammad's ﷺ life

my heart aches to be
with Sayyidina Muhammad ﷺ:
rose thorns in my palm

young Naseem inquires,
'how we can lay down and sleep
each night with strangers?'

The *dergāh* still dark,
praying voices merge with snores
from paradise dreams

on a back road, Lefke, Cyprus,
a small wood structure
is the world's safe house.

Unseen, Maulana's
peace arranges everything,
holds our soul's progress

someone's dimmed the lights,
we can see the dawn filter through
shadows in *sajda*

down in the valley
an earth mover's beat, a rain sparrow,
as sunlight returns

some glow aches inside
that matures toward darkness
toward greater light

three-hour *salawāt,*
these fragments of reality come
to bury Caesar

a passing woman
offers *salaams*: three of us
in wordless rapport

on an outdoor tap
as if awaiting sunrise
a perfect drip lingers

I puzzle who tagged
these words: me or Maulana
or God's Messenger ﷺ?

the most far-reaching
arrangement and the best word
is the work of Allah ﷻ

Abdur Rahman dives
into an ocean of recitation,
unknown words are wings

through open windows
centuries walk by in costume,
fresh faces address you

he's no 'anti Christie'
says kind intense Hisham—a red
swirl round his turban

he turns and instructs
me in *rakat*'s exactitude
as light fights each fringe

a tiny red rose
with *Hajj* pin on a turban
lies on Ibrahim's suitcase

in *Sayyidi*'s orchards
we pick olives around bees
with a donkey's kick

passing a penned bull
Abdul Wadud says 'moo moo'
with inflated ohhhs

snakes and ladders chalked
on the gritty kerbless road—
almost teased away

two huge serving boats
rice and stew: by high palm trunks
perhaps still grieving

white Jasmine flowers,
overhead constellations
exude their fragrance.

THE MOSQUE OF SEVEN COMPANIONS

Built on low rocky seashore—when Greek Cypriots dominated the area the mosque was reduced to a household residence; it now stands restored to a maqam or sacred site.

Inside Hazreti Ömer Mosque, you—
twenty-five years a covered Muslim—
and I—five days from my *shahada*—
submit before the tall green alcove
its unfigured hollow topped with
calligraphy you wish you could read.

The Mediterranean's cadences
sound through beats of thought.
Breakers could snarl and hurl
storm-froth on the shelter's roof
yet no weather-mood can perturb
seven green turbaned saints inside.

When, from eight centuries of warring
empires, Ottoman foot soldiers ducked
into a cave and chanced on laid-out
unaged bodies of seven companions
they appeared no more than children
cuddling for warmth, ready to awake.

The mosque's far-eyed attendant
collects for the abstract-bordered
sajjada we buy. Then, off duty,
discreetly steps out and taking a rod
casts for what he might discover
in rolling turquoise brightness.

In darkness, I see unknown mountains
enveloped with evergreens, curl
toward seven bare-stone summits
each wrapped in unwarpable
brilliance. You, standing close by
recite Arabic—*Ya Sīn*.

Slow that cosmic prayer moulds
the shore-rocks of our grief and love.

IMAM OF THE EMPTY MOSQUE

AW had asked, 'How are you?' Like any genii in a bottle responds to whomever rubs and summons it from retirement, his entry had been simple. The *murid* now followed the Imam in *asr* prayer. AW had hoped his visit would be pleasurable for the leader, breaking the boredom of non-attendance. But this wasn't the impression the Imam gave. In a contrary vein, the near endless thinker, AW, wondered if he took the Mosque up under his arms and walked away would this only stir the Imam to get in his car and drive to his next appointment? The lacklustre prayer dawdled on with precision and sense of complete disinterest. At the conclusion when AW would have gladly, reservedly, of course embraced the tall somewhat stiff Imam, a timid fish out of water, no, a handshake was enough—thank you! AW, an upstart in the Shaykh's domain, was constantly disarmed by how the mass of Muslims acted the opposite to Sufis and how those turban-wearers, beard-strokers, baggy trouser mortals performed everything in manner at odds with the conforming hordes. The Imam, pleasant but in a way suggesting that AW would grow out of his exuberance, outlandishness, and gradually be greyed over and calmed down outwardly and inwardly. So the head man patiently bore AW's attack of happiness (or was it insecurity?). AW blamed his insensitivity before he got out the door and thought of retracting, apologising to the Imam, but couldn't imagine what to say to convey his sadness at his deplorable conduct or how to say sorry—sorry for what? His supposed misdeed couldn't shake him across the threshold again and knowing the Imam's likely rapid departure there wouldn't be time to consider the universe and our state of innocence or guilt. Such sincerity would have annoyed this urgent servant of the state. AW would have offered a quasi-sorry, but the man was too quick for the nimble-minded novice. If he had succeeded, he would have convinced the Imam that AW was more unwired than imagined and that if this strange progression continued, he would have come to the final point that AW was dangerous. And in some relationships in the past AW had pursued such a timid course in his dealings of going from one act of minor lunacy to another that the victim at last deemed him deranged and by the most incontrovertible logic—AW was an enemy of the state.

SPRING ZIYÁRA IN NORTH CYPRUS

By St. Barnabas—
thready stems—wild anemones
in winter-rain's green

round last gospeller
filigree fennel and whites'
otherworldly mauve

two rough dogs won't bark
sniff attention and accept
bread in two torn chunks

one soldier in love's
truest colours will vanquish
a valley army.

In Famagusta
just a green-painted high kerb—
underneath a saint

'A Weeping Grandfather'
our youngish impromptu guide
says 'that's all we know'

his broken English
seems in mourning that he can't
communicate more

he recalls a truth—
how one night a fresh stream gushed
from arid sandstone

where passionate poor
found relief—the carer's name
lost—is remembered.

At Qutub Osman's
on his night house's pitched roof
I imprint my face

wood gives a little
under green gold-fringed linen
calligraphy plied

short-cropped narcissus
(water gone from a glass vial)
in a side alcove

detesting envy
I unlatch the grilled window
to release a fly

back by the green kerb
I kiss the chipped paint surface—
a body entombed

a fragrant Islam
under a Byzantine arch
black with candle smoke

how many drivers
have stopped, stepped out, prayed here
for the unborn child?

Their young wives' desires
resonate, asking help in
misspoken *du'as*

who dwells in kerbstone
man or woman, time-savaged or
fresh as windflowers?

With no lips to touch
that secret buried one's kissed
so many bruised lips

unknown, behind mesh
three martyrs' headstones intact
cuddled by green cloth

holiness remains
holiness—from Scroll—or Cross—
or Qur'an-bearer

in city racket
the undefiled is the pole that—
links us to Allah ﷻ.

Sense a loving grip.
From his night house, arms expand
to warm intruders

between sacred sites
Beshparmak cliff-profiles rise
as a last *maqam*

by churning blue-grey
in a cave, seven were moved
nine centuries late

still in bloom their cheeks,
their limbs, air just gone from lungs,
red shale clothes sweetened

our Paradise age
33 years—for the stillborn
for one past ninety

what's the green tint that—
as a *dhikr*-ing heart grows—
cleans the inner eye?

against rocks, the sea's
sway, swish and thump in our ears—
we plunge to *sajda*.

Death will snarl at us
but those whose hearts are love-scoured
when banished, will stay.

ENTERING THE LAND

AW and his companions knew Maulana's kingdom was beyond affairs of state and its dare for dare mentality. His empire no one but a few knew it existed. And yet Maulana had influence here. He'd crossed the border to meet a current Pope and pass on spiritual reassurance. The driver told a tale of how another cabbie had been caught speeding and was pulled over. The hand-held camera had registered 30 kph over the limit. When the policeman approached the car he saw that the man behind the wheel wore the Sufi gear of a Maulana follower. The driver facing the huge fine was let off without being told why. The magician's escape had been claimed as a Maulana miracle; the master had said on another occasion 'I am the police.' Knowledge of this escape didn't slow down their driver tonight. His extended sighs and *Subhanallah*s suggested that wearing representative clothes could make trouble as often as solicit favour. But the Shaykh was here now. They believed that. In the speeding mini-cab with them, coming to the border. The Shaykh had crossed the Forbidden Zone to visit Hala Sultan. The way to that female martyr's shire-mosque was signposted in sight of Larnaca airport. This companion (auntie) of the Holy Prophet ﷺ who came to conquer the Green Isle, still dispensed more than across-the-counter cures. She was a beautiful thorn in the Greek side (excusing a Christian metaphor). The Greeks had wanted to commercialise the vicinity, imagining perhaps the ultimate neon triumph, but no structure or business lasted long. The fourteen century dead female-soldier wouldn't tolerate anything unholy—no matter how bright—in her gaze or hearing. The South Cypriots retaliate by closing the mosque early, at 4pm, suggesting they have the matter under control (perhaps implying they own the place), when they have long conceded they don't. The rumour has circulated that the Greeks want to unload the shrine's jurisdiction to Maulana Shaykh.

The holy man, born near the place, used to visit to see his grand-mother, he told his amazed and worried family. AW had once entered the structure, its dome aligned with the tall palms' big-fanning sweeps; minarets rising behind graceful green; a vista across a dry-bottom lake, her *maqam* surrounded by mewling cats. Hala Sultan, in the Muslim army, as soon as she had reached the island on its first landing beach, fell from her horse and died. Her misadventure belies the spiritual strength that radiates from her small mosque that survives all recurrent upheavals. AW came inside, down various corridors, then he stooped under an emblem-framed doorway. When he entered her room his heart clung to the martyr's tomb, apparelled in soft calligraphy. Every subdued pattern became more and more profound. On her grave's Ka'aba side AW encountered the most otherworldly force. He knelt and absorbed a holiness' perfume. He remembered the story of the *maqam* keeper who reported he frequently observed her person draped in her own sweet light. What did the Shaykh see, as a boy, when he responded to his enquiring family, 'I've been visiting my grandmother,' AW asked himself, still staring out the mini-cab's windscreen. There's always a greater sight than the one you call yours, he concluded once more, for the hundredth time. His question lingered without an answer. He puzzled too how many Greeks could not resist the temptation and had to step inside Hala Sultan. He didn't speak his wonderings, letting them sink like deflated balloons vanishing inside himself. Abdul Wadud experienced a half-vision. He saw Maulana's face mirror a brilliant humility which grows to a reality and power that's beyond anyone's telling. As the master had said, so often, 'O people, stop being cheated by all the bright fascination of the worldly, and wake up to your spiritual destiny.'

FIVE SUMMER DAYS

the moon—
Muhammad's ✿ face
reflecting Allah ✿

*

few then many
returning crows roost
on a date palm

insistent cicada—
all that loud sawing
and not one branch cut

*

Mediterranean's
bubbly surf—pebbles roll
in and round toes

bathers play far off
on a ship's sunken deck
ankle-deep in dancing blue

*

huge owl strikes through
the orchard's low branches:
at last sleep's my way

*

lurking round corners
Jasmine's perfect scent
in broken-down Lefke

gradually calm
before moonrise—sharp-winged
cicada cease

in a lengthening train
black ants start to snake up
this white-walled house

*

on way to worship
at a Hajji's beautiful tomb—
unarmed soldiers greet us

a mansion dog howls
Gentlemen of the Night waft
the air with pleasure

don't pick the sweet fruit
from any graveyard tree—
Shaykh Efendi commands

*

heaped up rubbish—
the homeowner fires his shoe
at a sniffing cat

we walk the valley
between distancing streetlights
until only stars

at last out of sight
we hold hands: tapered shadows
beyond far-parted glows

summer stars trickle:
we passed by here in winter—
the wadi's rain-roar.

WITH THE CHILDREN

The Shaykh lived down a narrow dirty walled lane, a mosque at its top entrance and then around a curve along a single track which passed by his front door on a sharp bend, no pavement or sidewalks, just a shared way with many potholes. His habitation no wonder; its front door's bottom left blue panel had been kicked in, not by force or anger, by endless child-intrusions. There were always rioting kiddies around, through and inside the house. Upstairs, at least one worn shutter hung at an angle. Youngsters raced outside; the door again banged and the panel splintered a little more. Fruit and vegetables were piled in crates outside the door to feed the large household and visiting *murids*. A *murid* would stand there sorting and cutting out bad parts and bruises. The Shaykh might come by, with his uncountable pockets in a long waistcoat and coat and plaid shirt, containing money, in rolled up notes, a cypress-wood *tasbih*, slim bottles of rose perfume more expensive than AW could guess and in another pocket—or scattered among them all—sweets for those raving youngsters; the boys, their hair gleaming, the girls, their curls covered by fine scarves bright as hibiscus. His deep hidden pockets like 'Captain Kangaroo' from AW's boyhood TV days; the Shaykh's pouches bulged. He would rummage around inside for so long until their naïve excitement burst. All the stuff visitors gave him, he held a short time until he passed it on to someone else, distributing a world of commerce through his weathered clothing. Children gathered, almost knocking him off his feet, yelping, screeching, as they had clustered centuries earlier around the Buddha or Jesus or Muhammad ﷺ. May Allah ﷻ grant them all peace.

BESHPARMAK COTTAGE AT KARAMAN
WITH A MURID OF SHAYKH EFENDI

In a swish no clouds
and mountains vanish
above Radhia's table.

She clears misty holes
in her smallest window
glimpses across the valley

stony ascents gone,
no limit; just sky and curved
breakwater glimmer

she pounds, strains and sieves
sweet edible ores
in each heirloom bowl.

NIKAH NIGHT

After all, it was a full moon evening and the anniversary of Rumi's death. So after booking a hotel room finally, one room, the two lovers were married by the seated Shaykh in front of his community in the crowded, brightly-candled prayer room. AW noticed the master's blotchy brown face, another blotch perhaps since he had arrived; but from the old widower's eyes he saw giant love glints, a gaze that transcended grief. AW was permitted to witness but knew he could never attain such a state of being. The Shaykh, like the best of beauties, acted as if he hardly was aware of his extraordinary power, pretended to be less than skilful. After the shortest service imaginable, AW wondered whether depth necessarily needed length or not, as the Shaykh played the soft-headed 'geezer'. He reached deep into pocket sacks of his well lived-in waistcoat, reached through another side slit, inside left, outside right, for the unseen; his woven caves and coves, inner chest alcoves, into a multitude of unknowns, layers of compartments, cavities, niches and soft wells—as many grains of sand on the shore, as many stars in the heaven, are the subtle ways of Maulana. Eventually, as if this antic was a desperate search for wealth that he had lost in the clothing's maze, and no doubt a teaching story, the Shaykh-cum-magician pulled out some rusty Turkish notes that glimmered as sacred signs for the new couple. And they were deliriously satisfied by the hard-found gift, if not a fortune. Perhaps the Shaykh was saying that marriage too is a quest through many moods; after exertions and failed expectations you are pleased with a little which is a great blessing to be excited, over the moon about a pittance, so the little becomes a fortune.

MARRIAGE SUITE

1. Near Girne (before our marriage)

Our escort's red beetle
gets a flat—we peel
and eat three oranges
picked from the ground.

Blue, dark slate, turquoise
roll in and break throwing
manes of white against
Crusader Castle walls—
honeycombed to coral.

Building sites around
grimy olive groves—new houses
creep up the sacred slope.

Jinn's mountainface unmoved
two whole days we've been
among Girne's dust.

2. After our wedding day

Purring pines go quiet
all night rain trickles
for spring in two weeks

silent smoke
circles evergreens
till under a spell

uncrackling
mist weaves
up Komando tepe

dripping—a shower—
night rounds the grapefruit
in a guest house garden.

Sofina's oval face
in fireglow—like the moon
before it was moon.

3. Above Girne

St. Hilarion—
a white-tuft robin watches
by ancient monk's cell

we climb the cloudy
stair-path—against advice
of those descending

a minute in view
the sinking sun enflames
Beshparmak peaks.

4. After staying in a motel rotten with fleas

For Sofina

You kiss me and—
Mediterranean foams ashore
with love in its heart.

You sing—swirling
turquoise waves—a kind siren
who won't shipwreck me!

5. At Cyprus' end of the world

Zafer Burnu—
two shorelines touch
a high marker groans.

Two sounds and tempos
undermine cliff-rocks
north and south.

Timid flashing eyes
a wild donkey glances out
through thorny climbers.

From the cape
islands broken away
dwindle to surf.

THE NAQSH

As if time was a loaded chest—
with moth's warm death hum and owl
screeches—past tomorrows open

as in tropical night Green Shaykh
speaks of journeys—seven years without
provision in His Lord's rucksack

between us on five low tables
Turkish coffees and sober biscuits
link under a soft-chinned moon.

'A sudden explosion'
he re-outlines that half-vision half-dream
how 'day and night will combust

to leave a new earth.' With each phrase
his green garments bulge to carry his fifteen
children, his sweethearts, his servanthood.

As if disciples, we seven
or eight strangers listen, before dispersing
make new love-vows.

He knows and we understand,
as a mosquito whines, his message of the world's end
is a secret to share with no one.

NOVEMBER AFTERNOON,
NORTH CYPRUS

Valley flies annoy my earlobes.
One pinking pomegranate hangs
in the failing breeze. A Jasmine-
petalled butterfly floats under
a white quick-descending sun
below a vine's scorched fringes.
On the mud-house's pathway
my wife's two black shoes rest.
The town reservoir's a puddle—
this the first day it could rain.
Sticky, garnet beads collect
in a basin, as she pries open
and peels back the inner fruit...
the *adhān* calling us to prayer.

A FRIEND OF THE SHAYKH

AW's thoughts became lost. Started to long to reach the Shaykh; to cross the road, bear the traffic, avoid slick black *dolmushes*, walk a negligible verge, the only pavement, across the bridge over the waterless *wadi* away from the Mediterranean. The *wadi* deep-rutted and gored from distant storms; clogged with old cookers, crates and fridges and tyres. AW found it hard to concede that such items had been washed down from mountain tops. The modern world grinned through speeding dimmed windows; he was seeking his ancient Shaykh. AW didn't follow a golden road. The Shaykh lived in the middle of chaos; not the worst kind. At any time a crazed young man with a twisted face might lunge out and ask for something. With a doom-urgent voice from a wrecked and nearly toothless gape, he'd shout, beg. AW had once given him a sweet; he snatched it. Ate it without taking the paper off. Then seemed to complain this wasn't it, but it would do for the moment, as if AW better work out soon what he really wanted, but there was no 'or else' in his caved-in expression, in the tone of his fountain-spurt of unknown words. Then his wretched form disappeared through a door in a high wall. AW couldn't see where he'd gone. Who finally comforted his desire, his asking? The Shaykh lived near, down the lane, grass trying to separate the track finding a root-hold in cracks or where the surface had heaved to reveal its earthly heart.

A SPRING WEEK WITH THE SHAYKH
IN NORTH CYPRUS DURING
THE PROPHET'S ﷺ BIRTHDAY MONTH

To Shaykh Nazim al-Haqqani (40th Shaykh of the Islamic Naqsh-bandi Sufi Order), a spiritual descendant of Jalaluddin Rumi

Maulana's green turban
carries all day a cluster
of white wildflowers

I fall before him
kiss his black leather-socked feet
taste salt in its grooves

beneath a date palm's
high compass—whitest iris
relate galaxies

day's static swallow
on a raisin drying mesh—
with needle tail-feathers

Apricot petals
fragrancing a prayer mat
lightly kiss the ground

by elderflowers
I'm almost mad—on the wing
irises in flocks

sunk in sun daisies
as if stepping towards death
I scan remote peaks

by Forbidden Zone
a small, gentle domed mosque
by martyrs' white graves

in the Shaykh's garden—
Muhammad's ﷺ crimson roses
with a hush unfurl

sunset clips Lefke—
freshest lemon juice in soup
before ablution

the next day, seaweed,
playful littoral children,
fish smells on clothing

longest extant vine
twists up by Asmah Plaj—
flags wave infant green

beyond the Carob's
leather leaves—a cliff wedged beach
after thunder's hint

from the café pier
twilit Mediterranean
a silvered turquoise

bedding in Parsley
some roll tender *lahmacun*;
eat ketchup with chips

tea-drinking *murids*
repose near the Shaykh's kitchen—
a rooster on its roof

attending faithful
prop up the saint by his arms—
his tartan scarf waves

Shaykh Efendi's glow
from failing ears his white beard
mounds a warm blotched face

a streak of madness
his sacred room booms with song
and jumping Sufis

in one gaze my heart:
each follower longs to be
absorbed in the Beloved

on an inlaid stand
two water glasses: the Shaykh's
and oldest *murid*'s

after the *dhikr*
a child offers from a tray
moon-nibbled sweetmeats

our master's grandson
at last shouts *Go home! Go home!*
to dazed worshippers

meeting the Shaykh's eyes:
pupils on fire in love-light,
rims wet with longing

in death or living—
where does his seeing come from—?
listen to the heart

at his old wife's tomb
her *maqam* each mother's grave
un-mourned through the world

blue, mountain iris:
one way the Med—the other
misted pinnacles

among ruined Carob
wind chases radiant grass
up towards Vouni

the site's keeper states
Closing time as if locking up
twenty hundred years

across the Warrior
an un-guessed *bul-whooo* comes and goes
in the Shaykh's prayer room

a last interview:
the perfect man's turban twirled
in garden rose scent

half-closed eyes witness
his Cyprus in shaded blue
below dazzling

white beard hairs entwined
as if a snow storm; he strokes
my now vanished chin.

AT PIR PASHA'S JAMI, LEFKE, NORTH CYPRUS

The south wind ruffles my white sleeves.
Disturbs high cypresses, scimitar-needled
pines, an eight-hundred year Oriental Plane
across the way. I've prayed in mosque porch.
Lowered my head in *sajda*. But now am unable
to rise it up. I remain fixed to its shabby rug.

All I can do is listen to the world around me.
Even the old Plane tree is somewhat cowed.
I know its lower bole's hollowed and scarred
with hunky knots split and blackened; scabbed
and re-scabbed it seems uncountable times. We

invaders and indigenous, since the Pasha's age,
have scabbed-over our losses time after time.
I think on a friend's wife: her early departing,
and twins un-born; futures hoped for, believed in:
we, unhealed, must grieve in endurance.

On the mosque's valley side, pointing east
Pir Pasha's tomb—a long sandstone trough
with surging trim—must catch the winter sun:
Pir Pasha, witness of the Prophet's ﷺ faith.
His white stone, now black from devotion;
from supplicants, with chanted *du'a*, who
fresh as when he was buried centuries ago
burn candles, seek his intercession to close
their wounds, to stitch the shattered heart.
Wax—pink, red, yellow and blue or cream
. tinted—drips into knobby incidental currents
our panting drapes over the obstinate stone.

In the carpeted porch entrance, my head
sunk and stuck in submission, I imagine
the fabric imprinting spread-out palms,
bent knees, pressed forehead, like henna.

Everything's changed. I should panic
and shout; but just take in faintly distant
traffic groans that recall a tor's cross-roads.
A bent signpost points the cemetery's way
among baby blue-shadowed mountains where
the gecko prevails with its disappearing tail
where a young wife's grave is always moistened
(water bottles wedged into a nearby evergreen).
And toffee-colour blocks, in proportion round
the still calming mound, are newly mortared
by a few caring hands. I've stood at her grave.

Below the Jami, into the dry *wadi*, through
the east screen's miniature windows I can
taste (it seems) oldest date palms, loaded
with golden fruit stashes in deep bows—
each like a rich sky-suspended fountain,
the emblem on the Pasha's scorched tomb;
his eastward end-stone, in Ottoman style,
displays grapes below his turbaned peak.
The martyr still gives to our community
many believe and pray by his inhumation.
Earth each season submits its resources
although this year many will have pleaded
for rain beside his cenotaph's curvy edges.
Its inside rectangular hollow speckled with
exhausted birthday candles and matches.
Outside, through waterfalls of waxy drips,
his panels cut with symbols, power and truth:
scroll tubes, his patient arm and open mind.

I hear irrigation ditches gush and burble
ancient at least as Pir Pasha's conviction
around and below the domed mosque. They
gleam and disperse in an elaborate network
between households, feeding orchards, gardens
our terrace groves, intricate as an electric grid
regulated, shared and rationed. Small iron gates
closed or opened, the water's routed with care
to preserve the Troodos Mountains' run-off.

I can't move. My wrinkled forehead rooted.
Bear sounds: my shoulders ache, my knees,
a penny whistle bird song comes and goes,
Turkish residents, patriotic or not, exchange
greetings; sharp and dim, childhood laughter
at recess. Then that sound-quarter's vacant
back to their nationalist lessons, I suppose.
A helicopter with its mad batter blades
carries its frank message across arid land:
'Life here depends on alertness or the Greek
Cypriots will attack and re-invade.' The Pasha's
shaded resting place speaks a mute language
many suggest they hear; listen by his bones.
I wonder too, on this dusty ground, if angels
washed his body, buried where he had fallen—
as conduits murmur against a resolute sun.

A few days ago my wife and I relaxed
under Murida's twelfth century branches.
We noticed deep indents in the leaves and
their curled margins. Casually she served us
a sweet rose water drink, chilled, and almonds
encased in dates, in date jam in glass date-
shaped dishes. She gave their Turkish names.
She lives over the road on the mosque's edge
she wanted to reach out to us two strangers.

Black hair tied back, every day she scrubs
down her forecourt chasing the Cypriot dust.
From her back veranda the Mediterranean's
turquoise responds to the cinder brown hills.
She titled him, Pir 'Osman' Pasha, '*Shāhid*'
as if she knew his family; was glad to live in

a broom-stroke's reach. I'm in a lattice cage.
Pale pines shiver, etiolated geraniums twitch
round the grounds from soil in stone-rectangles.
Yesterday my hands rubbed their curly leaves.
I smelt on fingertips that familiar pungency.
Those hands shake as my arms buttress up
like a super beetle's shell my back's weight.
The bridge of my nose and forehead impress
the figureless carpet as if one postage stamp

in the dark. Until I shut down my eyelids,
peer inward, past blankness and alarm, watch
serene engulfing purples, crimsons of rare pitch.
Now, like someone stoops, looking in a pool
but doesn't see his reflection, but some other,
a strong forgiving face looks up from fathoms

with eyes grooved with love like sweet gems
or almonds, two openings to impossible greens.
And from a neck's V-shaped chain, below his
bearded skin, luminous as summer's noon sun,
a stitched cloth pouch dangles. I must stand
up on my feet and go about my business...

Yesterday, the father-sufferer, who had lost
two infants, still childless after some years,
arrived at the hillside mosque to make *du'a*.
Before I could mouth a word, he'd vanished.

But catching a side-glance I called out to him
passing in his plush car. He halted by the gate.
To my laboured query, he almost aggressively
responded, 'No it's not mine... it's a rental'
and drove off down the twisty narrow road
under the hanging hordes of ripening dates.
If not sure, a robin's song comes in range.
Maybe it's a cousin, a visitant or a migrant.
I can't budge. My long removed lace-up shoes
must puzzle where my feet have wandered to.

The first day I prayed here, two workmen
entered; loosened off their white-filmed boots
and performed *salāt* by me in their lunch break.
Fulfilling the old obligation, they left quickly.
In the afternoon, I heard their cement mixing.

Next day I waited on, past one, past two
at 2:45, a mid-age man shifted up the steps
in a short-sleeved plaid shirt, sand trousers,
with a cough that choked his brief greeting.
He unlocked the north's immense green door.
I followed him, inside, under five archways
a mellow stone niche, the *mihrab*, faced south.
He relaxed in a pillowed, east window chair,
settled a snow white prayer hat on his head
and read from a huge, stretched open Qur'an.
Ready to rise, he lifted the now closed tome
kissed and patted it on his tanned forehead.
Then, checking his watch, he rose and walked
over the rugged floor. With a cored microphone
he voiced the *adhān*, for *asr*: a small power box
by the niche's pillar. We heard his modulations
open out across valleys to the Mediterranean
from the loudspeaker-ringed minaret.

(A shaft, pointing up with a coned top
my wife and I fascinated late one night
the sky crowded with attendant stars)

The Imam robed in a hanging, black cloak
then enacted obligatory and *sunnah* prayers.
No other worshipper in the retiring shelter
I copied his lead, bowed and stood in turn.
Then with a *salaam* I followed him outside
into the verdant screened porch. He turned
back with keys jangling and locked the door.
Minutes later, drove off, offering a half-way
courteous goodbye through his rolled down
window—his bald head shining with summer.
Now, the door stands—twelve bolts in three
rows with two large metal rings—a barrier
where I can't crane my neck to observe.

I yearn to stare through its immense disused
keyhole and watch in front of a distant alcove
the turbaned Pasha enact extended prostration;
perhaps not in this building but some structure
when palm trunks were still notched columns
under a bamboo leafed roof or under the stars,
beneath the floor—a buried Byzantine church.

I hear our host, Murida, beyond the north steps
behind me. Her voice, slowly elevating to insist,
orders one of her three daughters to do a chore; her
black hair tied back, under long-spreading shade.

At last, with no logic, my head's free. I can re-
gain my feet, stand and gaze through the keyhole
if I choose or through lattice shimmering facets.
Under three arches: a westward, one on the north

elevation and one eastward, from all three views
diamond light-sections show the world in abstract.

And then, a breath, unexpectedly clamorous, rushes
through the porch and down to the grove gardens
where, as if earthless greenery, high fronds sing.
This wind, a pre-thunder gust, grows more stern
set to blow existence off its axis. Except, I believe,
our sorrows and loves will, like the Pasha's, stay
long after each Armageddon has come and gone.

OUR HIDE-AWAY

On the outskirts of Lefke, Cyprus

Standing I heard perhaps
for the first time that first dawn
my grave calling

your eucalyptus
gathered all the mountain winds
in its still green roar

a black mare galloped
silver trappings sparkled
over Troodos views

encompassed by mist...
a cloud gave birth
to snow-patchy peaks

no longer overcast
green slopes finally dulled
round our hide-away

our home chores lengthened—
'kindle water, scrub in bowl'—
each time's occupant

needing discipline
if we could stand discipline
on a squatty toilet

no one would disturb
swinging from the wire clothesline
my two old grey socks

slow an ornate flame
in our kitchen—your stitchwork
secured the window

you said, 'I wish you—
wouldn't write, live each day's page
elegantly with me'

I whittled the point
to how penning words helped me
stay sane each moment

yet there's a practice
to seek: the heart enlightened,
no need to record

a lizard's plaid head
peeked from crumbled mud-work
round our south window

the woodburner tinkled
as olive-scented smoke
roamed over our bed

the back of my hands
punctuated with bites—your spine
and hip ached from cold

our pathway lit up,
a lamp with floral iron threads
in Sultanate style

twice I tried to expel
through a gap over the door
a big black beetle

indoors, a handmade
pine wardrobe's Art Nouveau curves
threw back our yearnings

our stray-cat trio
chased by my bamboo besom
didn't once meow

one almost as tall
geranium with jasmine...
February perfumes

prickly pears kept up
their dead slow march down the hill
toward our rose patch

like crumpled bedding
mountains faded into blue-
grey-greens, silver-pinks

our sky's outdoor roof—
overhead grapes could mature
sun-creased to raisins

a grove in Prophet 🌿 green:
the year's oranges plumped into crates
from stained pickers' hands

on one valley walk
a soldier picked from the roadside
a white narcissus

a pill-box and flag
looked over us each new day
till just ornaments

through a blue hole
in a dark afternoon
we misread the sun

cowering from rain
in an affectionate pile
sticks broken and chopped

after thunder drops
under frail flashes, quietly
we approached our hide-out

'don't tell anyone...
where we are...' cupping your hand
round my ear's swirl

on a spiky tree
one dark pomegranate shell
like a strange charm

south wall a sun-trap
at night the Great Hunter's sword
pointed to the Ka'aba

a thousand before,
we unfolded prayer rugs
in shared seclusion

first light's *adhān* rose
from Pir Pasha's, we strayed out
to make hard *wudu*

a night-calling bird
at last silenced, expecting
a sparrow's chorus

everything that exists
has its blessed place, I guess
we'll return sometime.

CITRUS SCENT

In sun, by the sensuous orange grove
half-seen two women collect firewood,
in olive green the gushing *wadi* gleams,
in their hands branches of old trees crack;
a few steps apart, they leave small heaps...

The mother's head covered in the old style,
her daughter's black hair, tied back, shines.
Her young dad was martyred before the war;
at a mountain's foot their terrace valley leads
up to the Forbidden Zone that parts two Cypriots.

Each bends to grasp their own ignitable wood.
Citrus scents ooze and dark eyes stay estranged.

THE NON-MEETING

All the world disowned the Shaykh. Not his face or statue anywhere. The instantly diving sun was almost cut in two, sinking so fast against a hill's curved blade. Suddenly the red ball bled and vanished. It witnessed the Shaykh. The whole universe breathed in his sanity in the midst of everyday bedlam. AW couldn't subdue his fears entirely. 'What had the incoming night to do with me?' he fretted. How can anyone be alive here a day, a second, and not wonder, amazed in despair at the vastness above and around us measly forms? Us a few notches high, a little wider at the middle; nothing of substance; just fluid between porous walls of skin; just scraps of being that come and go like discarded pieces of paper the wind takes off the beach and throws in the water before it discolours and sinks. AW will ask the Shaykh when they meet why he thinks human beings have any importance when we're so small and dismissible. AW could hear his answer before he arrived. In silence between bursts of cicada as they slowly wound down for the night; before the crickets started. The master would re-phrase the question, hand it back like transformed fruit. 'How can a human being know their place?' he might ask, leaning on his walking stick-cum-magic staff. His frame jittery, a breeze could wrong-foot him, tie his legs in knots. His hands looking without the power to turn on a tap. Until he places his right palm on a *murid*'s head, in blessing, then his hands seem like King Kong's paws. AW called him to himself, 'King Kong of the Spirit'. Then his radiance would focus as he turned enquiry into revelation. Perhaps said: make peace with misfortune and you'll have fortune; overcome hatred and you'll receive love. Yes, AW chirped almost aloud, excited, as another night-glassed *dolmush* hurried past. The universe is not only to be examined. It's a model: how we should live unstintingly. The numberless not feared; embraced like a poet's endless verses. Let's be small and great. AW walked dust-calm grass and pebbles, changing one side of the road to the next, towards a half-planned meeting, that seemed a heart's rendezvous with no need for it to happen.

LEFKE, WINTER SEQUENCE

December breathes out
spring flowers yellowing
irrigation routes

collecting in
sunny corrugated grooves—
fallen pecans

a jingling stream's
upbeat music blends
with warbling *adhān*

a green and lemon
woollen Pakistani shawl
on an outdoor hook

a Sufi offers
a mandarin—its peel's scent
on his fingertips

the sun almost gone
behind Guest House's ruined car
overgrown with buds

at early *isha*
the full moon is too large
for the winter sky.

AT AHMAD'S ADOBE HOUSE

In unhindered sun
date palm's under-branches gold—
blue drips on windows

slowly death departs
from the house—more gradually
some last hint of her,

never sparse with gifts
on wrists, ankles, neck—red wounds:
mossies have come calling.

Who knows? A wild stretch
and stars could be higher fruit
on weighed down branches.

Still he tries—the Shaykh
too an old man growing old—
his voice from upstairs.

PEACE BE UPON HIM

You prayed, alone, in a mountain hole
through shrill night. No voice responded.
I pray in darkness in my walled-in heart
among ageing ambitions' heaped junk.
You knew unending illiteracy of being
and struggled through doubts, delusions,
before the Angel spoke; before converts
and fleeing for your life; the miraculous...
you lowered your covered head into rock
centuries had swirled and howled to sand.
Your daughter time to time brought food;
some Mekkah dates with well water I imagine.
You bowed not knowing light would come;
submitted against fear's rush. What beasts
might emerge? With lit eyes they perhaps
watched, waiting to see if you'd retreat.
In an absent room, my prayer mat glows
a rectangle of sanity; on knees I shake
repeating *salawāt*; through my fingers
a *tasbīh* rattles. From inside, faces gawk,
hornless devils or angels. More than past
your presence: is my quaking your doing?
You prayed bookless, no script written, your
knees imprinting glints. Before the mission
announced or you were entitled Messenger,
you felt emptiness; heard claims of lunacy—
everyone's distracting alarm; but yet went
on in worship before the Angel at last spoke
Read. 'I can't read' your humble words back.
When you slid down the scree and later told
Waraqa your vision, you looked in disbelief
that you would need to arm yourself with God

A LAST DAY

Waiting for Maulana.

For a murid one of the most cherished times is the final interview
with his beloved spiritual teacher before returning to the world.

Who am I, coming
to see the one who has stood
in Allah's Presence ﷻ?

My Shaykh? My turban's
white cloth newly washed and wrapped
tightly in woven folds

my fingernails trimmed
and white straggly beard perfumed;
wearing my best clothes

I do not know why
I'm welcomed by this Great One
his perfect gaze on me

I wait for the time
to be called: a pigeon coos,
Mosque sparrows cheep.

Waiting, that's the truth
who knows what will happen,
what love he'll impart

a Cyprus morning greys—
high oranges turn to ornaments
in the windless afternoon

on the quietest table
bold knots in grains have blackened
under varnishing

through metal fence spears
round the ground's white painted trunks
a weedy green stills

am I who loves
learning to wait for his Beloved
to serve the Unknown?

the Spring air cooler:
high windows won't be swung out
if his front door's open

this head's too heavy
for my arms' support; my elbow
slips off the table

a big, blue-jumpered
Majnun talks in Turkish, then calls
for 'money, money'

a young sightseer
(I don't know) with a big lens,
kneeling, frames a weed

the wall hasn't shifted
an inch in the last two hours...
perhaps my Saint sleeps

chirps, trills and whistles
an excitable bird flits
round a huge-coned pine

sweet almond blossoms
don't fret with littlest wind
to tickle them down

the Lover foresees
but it's past imagining
meeting his Beloved

two butterflies prance
as if one—from my sightline—
above photo's green

a white prayer hat
with his swinging shopping bag
a *murid* passes

a spider web broom
leans with its bristles upright
in the Mosque's west corner

a cute-faced mouser
who tagged me yesterday
hasn't slinked round today

at Maulana's door
even one broken orange crate
looks like a barrier

asr calls:
maybe I've missed my chance
feel a moment's fear

think: I've misplaced
some vital condition
to be given entry

bergamot lemons
on an oval dish might reach
my Shaykh before me

favourites who keep watch
might drive him to the mountains
after his long rest

The Lover can't see
each mischance skilfully fits
to make an opening

just as all hope dims...
I'm invited up to his room
to pray at his right side

The Lover distrusts
Love, can't believe his Beloved
would let him breathe so close

Maulana takes up
my right hand, slides a green agate ring
down my forefinger

too nervous to face
his warm mottled face, hardly grasp
his un-worlded beauty

ancient and present
his chest breathing rough and smooth
from his big blue armchair

his hand rests on my life
blessing journeys and family
giving a new name

I don't want to leave
lag behind hoping to catch
another gemstone.

His eyes say: 'Go out
go out; but keep my miracle
in your *dhikr*-ing heart.'

Creeping through the door
I long to hug everyone
stand and chant my faith.

After the Beloved's touched
I'm given power to submit
to his blessed presence.

THE SHAYKH AND THE DEAD BABY

Omar wrapped the baby in a blanket and carried it to the Shaykh's door. Omar hoped for a miracle; the Shaykh had saved others. An attendant answered. Omar said he wanted to see the Shaykh and have him touch his dead baby. 'That's impossible,' said the attendant, 'he's grieving the death of his wife; any more grief would be unbearable.' He turned Omar away. Omar started to walk. Who knows how long he would be carrying his baby covered in a tender blanket? Omar couldn't go back to his wife. He couldn't face her sorrow; he knew, though he didn't want to, he would blame her for the death. He had to keep walking; there was nothing else to do. No one paid attention to him trudging along busy hot streets, stopping now and then for shade. At least once, probably more, he pulled back laps of the blanket to stare at his baby: maybe she'd be breathing. He looked at her purple mouth and locked eyes, holding her stiffness gently. He closed up the bundle and started to stroll. A friend saw him and came over and asked, 'What are you doing? You can't carry a dead baby around forever you know.' Omar stopped and was polite but unmoved. His friend disinclined to drive the point home, quickly left Omar to his perambulations. The mourner walked on through exhaustion and wretchedness. Where was he going? There was nowhere to go. At last he began to think about the Shaykh and his disappointment that the 'great one' couldn't help. He had been his only hope. But gradually Omar considered the master's sorrow and started to feel for his bereavement. He decided to make *du'a*. Finding a secluded place not far from a mosque and placing the baby with great care onto the ground, he began to pray for the Shaykh. Who knows for how long he was on his knees with raised, cupped hands? Omar forgot everything else; concentrating more and more, his heart was drawn toward the Teacher's heart. At last Omar came out of his reverie and looked down. To his astonishment his bundle and baby had vanished. He feared a dog might have come along and snatched up his child. But it was unthinkable that he wouldn't have noticed such a thief; or perhaps some local trouble-maker had taken it. But no, he would've surely heard any such disturbance. Of course, he also thought that wherever his baby might have gone, it must be alive.

RANDOM SEQUENCE IN THE HOLY PROPHET'S ☵ BIRTHDAY MONTH, FEBRUARY 2011

Men and women chat,
at last the iron gate's open
to the orange grove

above oxalis
morning migrants flit here, there,
before turning north

inside his iron cage—
the moment our pupils meet
the dog halts barking

on a breakfast tray
five wind-fallen small oranges
with a pungent scent

I ask for grapefruits,
slow, the server shakes her head
guessing I love them

someone gives someone
a cute Peter Rabbit mug—
nearly in friendship

on the Prophet's ☵ birthday
there's a pink ring round the moon
foreshadowing rain

the fruit hardly picked
hanging angel trumpets and lemons
in a kerb garden

a young sister sniffs
a rose—almost revealing
'it's like her perfume'.

From her dead mother
a girl's red *tasbīh*—frays, snaps
under night fireworks

helpless—she recovers
84 beads in moist grass
before the Spring rains

winter morning glare
her best clothes lie scattered through
the house—like feathers

how can all these clouds
release so little?—I ask
my fellow brothers

sweet, spiced, long-cooking
Pakistani tea—just right
after the *Mawlid*

whether or not we'll
see—Shaykh Efendi—who knows—
rose in his turban

the watch dog's been tamed...
I stroke his ear—his brown eyes
carry the new moon

pocked as an old face
one picked orange among many
to be smuggled home

the stone arch over
Maulana's door—I've noticed—
displays one flower

into the mountains
some seek his trail—others wait
to be invited

dusk on close summits—
dark blue on blue—come morning
a distant slope's haze

I kiss Muhammad's ﷺ
beard hair, bow my head on it,
kiss its holder's hand.

MY SHAYKH AND WATER

Seated. His right hand surrounds a glass.
One straight finger raised toward Allah ﷻ
he hands on the water to his followers.

He didn't, in the past, point toward heaven
when taking a sip. But now he does, finding
new ways to worship, to better remember

in each act, His Lord. Each *jum'a*, after talk
he passes on spring-clear fluid he has touched.
And some take a sip. Others down it whole.

FORGIVENESS

Why should a holy man want to see a worm like him, (full of contention) AW concluded, the newly arrived. In the small Sufi mosque or *dergāh* where Maulana past 90 years of age would make his weekly appearance, the turbaned prayer-hatted brothers were already gathering. Many had slept there, rising for night prayers then *fajr*. Now they prepared for *jum'a*. Their rolled sleeping bags stashed in various back corners. AW saw an old young friend, almost forgotten, near the front where Maulana would sit in his wooden, floral upholstered chair. AW softened. He asked if he could join him. The beautiful-faced youth from a sub-continent background more British than AW, smiled a pleasurable yes. When Maulana arrived, about an hour later, more than once the aged Sufi master gazed at his weak servant, Abdul Wadud, at his malcontent, and touched his heart and mind, without forcing a confession. The deep eyes in his Shaykh's slumped face, full of power and humility struck AW and only then did he accept or believe he'd entered Shaykh Efendi's Realm. With little fanfare the night traveller had arrived.

May Allah ﷻ forgive me, forgive them, forgive us.

BETWEEN TIDE-LINES

A boy and his young sister and I struggled between
tide-lines on a North Cypriot, out of season, beach; pebbles and
rotund stones and 'skimmers' had been tossed in heaps, with
each step our shoes dug in we gave up half a stride.

We played hide and seek among surf-edged eucalyptus;
with eyes closed, I counted while the two siblings sought a good
hiding place; they crouched behind the boldest trunk with
initials carved high and low in its too tender bark.

Neither made it 'home free'. In no time, I spied them.
Light dulled; the foreshore moaned; pebbles were muscled up
the beach then forced back into the next wave's in-rush. With
each blue-turquoise turning a long hissing white

I saw perched, on a sea-ringed boulder, my old Shaykh
his green turban riffled, his spring *jubba* buttoned to the chin.
At the core of his world-cuddling love, he sat in seclusion. I
gave distant *salaams* and pictured 'an ocean in an ocean'.

THINGS LEFT BEHIND ON AN ISLAND
PILGRIMAGE PICKED UP ONCE MORE

Him, puffing his Camel
me, my *tasbih* on the swing—
what's the difference?

Cypriot lemons
in a near-midnight bowl
can calm a bee sting

A polished glow—
thunder without moisture
through late afternoon

No breeze can perturb
through legions of high reeds
a weak-chinned moon

From a friend's *salaams*
loveliest stars shine
on my long hike home.

Best life is like a rose—
once we appreciate
its beauty we accept
without reproach its thorns

One by one I kill
mosquitoes as the incense
burns in a blue jar.

Trees could be black clouds
from sandy brown mountains
the orchard crackles

Above two chess players
the full moon's found a partner—
an elusive star.

Before a check-mate
each remembers Muhammad ﷺ
a Mercy to the Worlds.

I don't dread time's end
but the crime that might
turn my Lord from me.

Maulana's asleep
perhaps awake, wake-asleep
on Allah's ﷻ duty.

Hourglass of black tea
for the dusk to dawn players,
time to pray *fajr*.

I carry a chair out
onto the buzzing porch
and do *salawāt*.

Curve-trunk palm holds
more than dates for one who stares
through its leaves to his heart

Eternal kindness
seems near yet far round these fields...
I stroll sometimes run.

The Creator's hush
deepening—at last accept
His command to sleep.

What, *Ya Wadud*
is Your secret—
is Your sweetest gift—
Your most tender good night kiss?

The pilgrim doesn't know
he's gone before he's died—until
he wakes in Your Love.

PART TWO

Perhaps a Final Sojourn
in Shaykh Efendi's Realm

I

Though AW had visited seven times before—dream or vision—arrival in Cyprus was more than his expectations. The rapid taxi drive from the airport—out the window the scarred landscape at first Greek, glass-fronted shops, the ancient land and modern land waging war. Suddenly AW, who had left Sofina at home, was in his lodging in a traditional adobe house on the Turkish side, thick walls, deep-set windows, wooden lathing on the sloped ceiling with cross-beams.

Late, he unpacked the necessaries, letting the rest stay zipped up until tomorrow. Before sleep he looked in the mirror and stroked his beard and saw the blotches on his face. Like those that had decorated his father's face and Shaykh Efendi's complexion, he thought. The Sufi novice was coming of age; he was nearing seventy.

> Silver diamonds
> across prayer rugs—moonlight
> through the lattice

Next day, returning to the Pir Pasha Jami, AW learned the tradition of pouring water from a glass on top of coffee in a small china cup. This gesture is performed before sipping the coffee to remind the drinker that Pir Pasha died, was martyred, from drinking poison in a celebratory goblet. His Greek enemies arranged both a triumphal display of delicious young women passionately dressed which distracted and charmed the general who took the victory cup offered to him without fear of treachery.

Three brothers sat after *zuhr* prayer on plastic white chairs with a tray of coffee between them with two full glasses of water. A spillage can occur when the coffee is well up almost to the rim. Yet each prayer-hatted *murid* tilted in turn one of the glasses and let the liquid pour on top of the coffee as if to neutralise the chance of being poisoned or to symbolise the need for humility always, especially when receiving a gift or being honoured. By design the water partially spoils the richer coffee.

irrigation troughs
gush-roar—below riotous
nest-builders

a lizard fades
into the shadows marking
an old olive tree's bark

AW's Maulana has passed away. The spiritual pole of the community died a year ago, that strength which gave support to so many in their weakness, who possessed perfect manners, whose love spread throughout the island and much further, but who lived in Lefke and shared with its population. The Sufi community has been wrenched by his demise. Later, on the first full day in Cyprus AW was being driven around the valley across the stone-dry *wadi*, past an ancient arch—in ruins but for the sublime ideal of curved blocks supported by a keystone. It stood isolated, its jagged margins' masonry and stones protruded into space, divorced of its connective purpose—remnants of a bridge, viaduct, a victory arch.

A friend drove Abdul Wadud on, a long-standing companion and fellow prayer-hatted Sufi, his hat a little faded. Everywhere was dotted with gorgeous coloured flowers, hollyhocks in cerise bloom beside last of flag iris. Or where a climber entwined an orange tree with orange globes draped with indigo blooms. They passed fields already arid and bluish-greens almost turquoise in that late afternoon May light; an olive grove, each tree spaced and well-tended. Passed the rundown, nearly fallen down houses, their underlayer of mud exposed and the new concrete walled dwellings with balconies and patios, usually flat-roofed angular structures. 'Heinous villas' another friend called them. The van's windows were down and birdsongs intruded: sparrows, swallows and tiger birds. In a convoluting way through villages, some never entered before, the twosome wound a passage towards the sparkling blues of the Mediterranean and also towards contaminated land, bulldozed into heaps from rapacious mining that operated a generation ago when the island seemed at the mercy of big business and mining companies who were indulged under the Greek control. AW's driver with his longer than he remembered beard, now definitely white, with his sincere expression broke the silence with, 'He asked me to give him water.'

AW's friend was referring to the Sufi master Maulana. AW didn't enquire if a dream or a vision, knew both were tenable. His companion suggested that the request had been very recent, since the master's death, and then he asked the newly arrived what he thought. AW offered a few possible interpretations looking out on the fawn land. Felt the strangeness in his friend's little white van used for hauling a family and cargo around, felt the almost queasiness of the master, holy man asking anything of one of his *murid*s, his followers, but AW could easily trust that Shaykh Efendi could demand, 'Give me water.' Maybe the perfect man was in need or maybe he wasn't. That was the delicate balanced issue—could a wonder-worker and saint have requirements? His driver and AW more or less concluded that their community was deficient and the master offered a remedy—don't forget me like a wilted plant; give me water, your attention. AW mused how he had been on the island in every season, first that winter, then roasting summer, then autumn and sometimes early spring and now this sojourn, neither spring nor summer, a May stretch of time. He, old man, young *murid*, marvelled there had been periods in his life too between seasons, between believable demarcations, between histories perhaps.

The Med drew near with a still expanse of blue that suddenly gave shape to the unconnected land, the island; now the interior had a skin, an outside, an exterior. AW could imagine being in a boat far past the surf lines and looking towards the shoreline of North Cyprus and seeing its form, mountain cliffs, bays and harbours; its particular contact with the sea through rock, pebbles, boulders or sand. But there would also be a perspective and in the same instance the island would be idealised into a creative shape, mould, the conflicting interior in that landward gaze would vanish, there would only be an outline, a membrane.

The *Qutb*, the pole of the age, had passed away, the greatest living representative of thousands of years of Sufi tradition and practice and wisdom was now contained, it seemed, within an elaborate casket deep in the *dergāh* covered with fabric inscribed with calligraphy as if he would need warmth against the outside's cold. The whole tomb slightly sloped towards the east, his turban tilted at one end. Many came to pay respects, give *salaams*, to the deceased. He had only had his life after all, nothing more could be added, not a day, and all his humour also smothered under green written layers of formality; his poetry, that way he spoke, teasingly direct and subtle—be soft-hearted, oh you no-mind people, the tricks and traps, the first hard-hearted was *Shaitan* and so on. If somebody does you one good deed it should take a hundred bad deeds before that one act of kindness is cancelled out. Many read from the Qur'an beside the master's *maqam*. AW's companion didn't go down to that complex of lodge, kitchens and family home; he stayed away and preferred to worship at the Pir Pasha mosque.

AW understood his aversion. Shaykh Efendi's place of remembrance was everywhere in the world; he could address you, request from you or suddenly stand beside in prayer anywhere. He wasn't bound to his ornate burial site. AW had a thought and eventually shared with his driving compère as they turned back toward Lefke, crossing the preliminary gap and surface that will become another expressway sweeping across the island. AW hesitated but looking across to his road-absorbed friend he said, 'We can't really understand our Shaykh unless we meet him person to person. How can anyone understand the poetry of Hafez unless they meet him or the teachings of Muhammad ﷺ or the spirituality of Jesus, for that matter, until you encounter them?'

His friend agreed. AW realised against most of the people in the world, he believed an unhindered meeting with these dated human beings, mystical entities, these lights of creations, was only a wave away at any time.

> He spoke of his shock
> his sad aching—for those who
> sink into the world.

II

AW was reluctant to leave his company when he parked up. The day was all but spent. The visitor knew the way to the *dergāh* and preparations for *maghrib,* the sundown prayer, but felt at odds with urgency or dependence on tradition. He'd go along the roads and down the lane past the cypress tree-curtained mosque to the Shaykh's heartland, his house and Sufi lodge and now *maqam* and see what would happen. Sufi brothers and sisters were gathering from around the world to commemorate the passing of Maulana and his love-light and to celebrate his life.

AW could meet anyone along the road or at the entrance of his house where the women collected or at the open doors of the *dergāh* where the men congregated and would be praying soon, the women upstairs with its squeaking floor boards and rampaging children—at least sometimes. The male Sufis prayed downstairs. AW knew this evening there would be pressure on space; people would perform *rakat* on benches, in doorways, in the forecourt on big unfurled carpets or make-shift mats and rugs. The building's small size suggested that a few could undertake this mendicant path, only a few could be guided by Shaykh Efendi. But worldwide he had touched some and now a good number converged on his little shelter-cum-sleeping-quarters-cum-sanctuary-cum-eating-hall to honour him and be touched by his memory. These phrases fail to convey the other desired possibility of being drowned in his actual spiritual presence. The longing and expectation would be at work in hearts. He may be more powerful, more approachable, some discussed, without his earthly self to carry around.

At the entrance to the small wooden building AW met a Sufi he'd known for years and with whom he had recently fallen out. He was selling bottles of perfume. AW knew they were exquisite, not artificial, understood something of the techniques he used with a tincture of love to find the best raw materials and create his bottled fragrances. Now here he was with a big hug dispelling latent discontent and, on his table, glinted rows of colourful petit containers of perfume. The Prophet ﷺ had said the three things he loved in this world were women, perfume and prayer. AW jokingly related to some trusted contacts that perfume was his alcohol, his liqueur, whiskey. Breathing *oudh*, jasmine or distilled rose or the dark euphonies of musk, its luring sensuality could inspire, entice, empower and subdue. The seller had grieved AW. The seller of fluid phonemes offered the chemistry that touching your skin carried the essence of the mystical, dream or vision. AW had his dreams and visions to display and sell, on his fragile stall and table, in books—but that would have to wait until tomorrow.

> For another year
> the Oriental Plane is out—
> who computes each leaf?

Existence will always have this ethic, it seemed: whatever union AW pursued will be tested like a rare document thrown into a fire. He'll have to pull it out and then read the original script. That is if his hands can tolerate fire, yank it out soon enough, if he can decipher what's lost... and he's dependent on others doing the same. Some bonded papers survive a lifetime.

> Eight empires from its
> planting—with a hollowed trunk
> it's in leaf, in seed
>
> a white tee-shirt
> has given birth to its
> first little hole
>
> Scops owl's shy *choo choo*
> calls the waning moon from
> beyond the mountains.

III

Playfully under the single street lamp in front of once Maulana's house in early evening, AW engaged with a girl child of about three, competing who owned the greatest imagination. The dark curly headed toddler drove a plastic wheel-based rocking horse. Its white plastic wheels groaned back and forth pushed by the girl towards the lit house entrance or in the opposite direction towards the lane's darkness. There was the common milling around of women outside the Shaykh's house, under its stone-arched threshold, now with a bite out of one floral sculpted tooth. The girl's young mother was content with Abdul Wadud approaching her daughter who had looked at him with some kind of expectation when AW was merely waiting not pre-meditating how to play with this spirited horse-riding child.

Cars as the norm also half-blocked the lane. She zoomed towards or away, forward or back along the rough tarmac. AW pointed out her habitual action to which she guided her horse sideways towards the cracked plaster walls of another series of less conspicuous dwellings, then spun her equine vehicle around and charged towards the other side of the road with its thin metal-post fence which enclosed the Shaykh's garden. AW's first serious move in this game was to stroke the horse's white plastic mane and admire the creature's features such as its strong head and nose. She quickly responded with her own impression, stating the beast possessed a big nose. AW called them nozzles. In the semi-darkness, child and man examined qualities of the horse further. AW celebrated its eyes and she replied with 'It has ears', gripping the protruding handles which she used to control its wheeled gallop. At the wrought-iron fence with the horse positioned towards the garden's flower displays AW suggested the sturdy toy might need feeding. She stepped from the saddle and undertook to give it nourishment with her small, cupped hands under the horse's mouth. A rich fragrance exuded from various flowers and AW wondered if her horse would like to eat that perfume. She commented that it enjoyed looking at the flowers in the Shaykh's garden. AW remembered once that Maulana defended the virtues of a certain black snake as being, 'A good one. Don't hurt it.'

The child stood confidently beside her vehicle-cum-horse with her dark curls, wearing a coat and wool leggings as the temperature had fallen after the sun disappeared. It was a night with little haze; the stars prominent. AW mooted the thought that maybe they could feed the horse with stars, perhaps he would like that, to which the pragmatic three-year-old retorted 'No' and after a puzzling pause asserted as if looking for a reason, claimed, 'The sky's too high.'

She implied that the horse was an earthling not a skyling. 'Too high,' she pointed upwards with her finger, giving a visual demonstration. AW came back that some equestrians have wings, so the sky is not too high. This brought another period of inaction and reflection which led to her imitating the neighing sound of her horse. She answered the problem with an intimate understanding of her toy's feelings; she spoke for the creature and its limitations. AW listened at this point in their game of inventive discovery, giving no indication he was convinced by her expert neigh.

AW's silence in the darkness under fanning beams of town light, he hoped would tease the child on. All at once, not in a logical leap, she gathered the potential of their playing into a potent statement. Stretching her arm up above her head towards the stars, she exclaimed and extolled, 'They are twinkling horses!'

Waving her hand across the span of the spotted cosmos. After this perfected fusion of ideas AW conceded that she was the imagination master, offering an imaginary bow. The child sat in the saddle and wheeled her pre-fab horse back towards the Shaykh's house doorway and her mother. The aged man started towards his lodgings at the south end of the valley, walking under fountains of palm fronds—in a street light gap—a star became a pendant among serrated shapes—a nugget of under-world beauty displayed in night's highest regions. Defeat was pleasing to imagine a child of three had sustained and cultured a metaphor and transformed it into iconic certainty—the twinkling horses. A peculiar lapse, AW hadn't suggested that the beast might require a drink.

IV

Each day except the first AW stood or sat at his table stall displaying his books for sale. His competitor had lined up perfumes and AW arranged his volumes of poems and short fiction dedicated to Maulana. Their pages described the vistas of Cyprus, changing seasons, the heat and cold, the Forbidden Zone, the island's dryness and rain, though often not a drop between May and October. Shaykh Efendi was portrayed as the centre, an elusive contact whose devotion and interest may spring far away from those enquiring. AW wanted to convey his experiences and impressions; those frequently unusual encounters between the Sufi master and himself and others that grew almost immortal in a protected mind-space.

The display table was wedged against the wall of the Maulana's house, under a green shuttered window with a crumbling stone ledge, graffiti cut into the plaster set to bolster an archway now vanished but for one pier. The books sheltered from the wind, rested in small piles, their covers slightly turned back, curled from the semi-tropical elements. Years had gone into their writing. Many visiting followers of Shaykh Efendi came up to the table, browsed AW's pages, commented, and some purchased the orphans. Carried them away. Later in the *dergāh*, AW saw a Sufi holding his book, passing it around, giving it significance, with the common expression, *Mashallah*, meaning, as God wills.

He experienced a subtle divide in his psyche observing his books externally handled, pages opened, stuffed into a *murid*'s wide jacket pocket, then re-emerging for a second reading.

AW's table disappeared on two occasions. He arrived on those mornings and had to search for his plastic board. He felt his presence was a minor irritation to some people. Whilst others valued his creative efforts, some found them a threat to their privileged view and association with the deceased Shaykh Efendi. Those, perhaps, closest in blood wanted to communicate that they alone had the right to present the Shaykh's importance, wanted to select what should be remembered. The old Sufi master, with his deep generosity, had acted as if he belonged to everyone. He had remarked that 'We are closer to the whole of humanity than our own families.' His elevated belief in humanity had inspired many, including AW. There was every probability that many other literary portraits would be published and distributed over the years ahead.

AW's stall encouraged many to reveal their experiences with the Shaykh, peculiar ways the master had come to a potential *murid* and drew him or her towards his high Islamic path of angelic manners and concern for all living things. The stacks of volumes were dwindling. The saint had made anyone feel special and at times he would single out a follower for criticism—by a facial gesture or a veiled joke. He had mirrored what his *murid*s needed, each one different yet vital. He angled his teaching with a level of respect so the student hadn't become defensive.

Some flipped the pages almost frightened to risk concentrating on the Shaykh, or perhaps the book stirred reminiscing that released concomitant strains of grief. AW had written to honour the Shaykh and had his permission to portray his person and action. 'Can I write about you?' the novice had once asked. The Shaykh looked up towards the higher otherworldly powers and looked back down towards AW and said, 'Yes.'

That gesture; his head tilting as he checked on a confidante in the ceiling of the room, in the space above, a witness, someone he could trust, who knew more than him. The ether around him confirmed the value of the request. At the stall, young *murid*s paused and began to read about the existence of Maulana, with various semi-precious stone rings on their fingers; their long-sleeved shirts, collarless, in stripes or plain; their turban or prayer hat could be in such a range of colours as if representing the many flags of the world. Their languages mixed. Some disappointed that the book wasn't in German or Turkish or French. 'No, English,' AW was forced to reply.

Two young females came up to the stall and enquired. The one dressed in a remarkable cloak with dainty flower patterns, black headscarf and swift eyes that ran across a few pages in each sample. She asked which was the author's most important and essential volume. Probing as if she tried to reach the heart of his enterprise. Her scrutiny confused him a little at least. AW couldn't answer effectively; they were all essential in some manner. Then the twosome moved on. Some overcame limitations and bought a copy. They pulled notes out of wallets, out of top shirt pockets, or out of a purse with brass clips, from an envelope, in sterling, US dollars or Euros, or in Turkish lira. AW puzzled what Maulana would have thought if he'd read his written words about meeting him. Would the master have withdrawn permission? In another case, an Asian wife sought AW's advice about her American husband—his poetic skill needed nurturing. A Portuguese planned to send AW examples of his English writing for him to refine and enrich.

Maybe it would happen? AW questioned his conscience. Sometimes managed to encourage a prospective buyer to read a whole poem that the poet worked out would impress him or her. Conversations led to insights helping him pinpoint a story or verse that might appeal. Some resistant to selling ploys enjoyed the exchange and dialogue, a chance to disclose their own worries and perspectives. Those twin innocent females that lingered over the visitor's stall walked by on numerous occasions without a word. One of them came back to enquire how AW's sales had gone. A quicksilver smile and gaze from under her *hijab* and she was away.

There was much to do: go to the *dergāh* to pray, the house for food and relax, meet favoured *murids*, go to Maulana's *maqam* to give *salaams*, read *Ya Sīn*, make supplication. In another moment while a middle-aged wife and her flamboyantly dressed sister scanned AW's table, her stalwart husband walked up and opened a sizeable wallet; after a briefing from AW he bought everything the two women had looked at. One way to keep their eyes in check, considered AW. Others promised they would return and did to obtain their selected item after going to a hole in the wall to secure cash or intent on waiting until the last day to make purchases. Naturally some promises were not kept. On various occasions, through first impressions, rapport grew between him and others. Sometimes giving *salaams* had a cumulative effect. Occasionally a follower bowed and kissed AW's blotchy hand as if the *nūr* of Maulana could be passed on. Lapsed friendships re-formed at the stall, and new commitments were forged.

Those published leaves were another way to nurture the community and the Shaykh. Love repeatedly the theme and re-reading the poems or stories the recurrence of that word struck AW. Faintly dismayed by its duplication, knew it was the irreplaceable glue that bound this global itinerant community together. One had to forgive a harsh word over and over. AW was tested over enough matters to feel his sensitivities stretch further to try to embrace every discontented person.

On the fifth day a middle-aged woman in elegant *hijab* with abstract trim offered a sequence of words in Arabic referring to the Prophet ﷺ and Allah ﷻ as an unfailing method to attract shoppers to his stall, of which many would purchase his things.

> pregnant clouds
> over blue morning glories
> groaning sky
>
> after the hailstorm
> a parade of bubbles
> down the street
>
> swallows swoop so low
> you can see the jewellery
> on their purple backs
>
> a curtain of rain
> from the *dergāh*'s eaves—
> now sporadic drips
>
> a drift of white clouds
> after thunder's rage
> and lightning's stab.

V

A huge ceremony had been prepared at Lefkoşa's cathedral-cum-mosque to commemorate the passing of Maulana. Seven buses were required to transport the Sufi community from Lefke to the capital city of North Cyprus. A hot, late afternoon, bottles of water were handed out. The pink blinds half-drawn at the driver's front windscreen and the light green curtains on a plastic cord fluttered across the passengers' windows. AW left his stall early and waited until the final coach arrived. Some *murids* had to stand in the aisle until the transport reached the depot some miles away where a mini-cab was also requisitioned for the exodus.

The sinking ochre revealed rolling fields of the plain between the mountains, their wheat already cut and the straw bundled. The slanted light exposed the rock textures of high peaks each with its pattern and size. It was past the city's rush hour when the group arrived and began walking through the narrow streets, most shops closed, towards the celebratory mosque. Past the disinterested city of sand-coloured Byzantine and Ottoman architecture, some buildings earlier and many much newer constructed in the last few decades. The company marched a small army of turbaned heads, swinging arms and flowing cloaks by drinkers in an open-air café and phone shops—one *murid* had to stop and test the prices.

It was *maghrib* when AW reached the precinct of the mosque crowded with the previous busloads but also with others who came from everywhere to honour his extraordinary Shaykh—like all religious leaders and citizens of Konya had come to the funeral of Jalaluddin Rumi eight centuries before. Now a host of mourners and bystanders filled the pavement at the building's east entrance where food was being served: rice with dates mixed in, yoghurt drinks, water, bread along with a variety of sweetmeats and pastries. Crash barriers were in place to direct visitors toward the food counters. The mosque's great arched entrance, its threshold awash with discarded shoes; big signs illustrated no shoes inside. AW had to find a retrievable place where he could stow his footwear among all the other shoes that had found perches among the tooled stonework or on provided wooden five-tier shelves.

Inside the vast structure undecorative columns held up the celestial roof, an immense carpet stretched into every corner and nook or swept away through the main section towards the mosque's distant west end. The men clustered towards the Ka'aba side, in various ante-spaces clearly chapels in the original plan and the women were packed in along the north wall seated in the same direction as the men. A low wooden rail distinguished the women's domain.

In between these divided ranks a big vacuum prevailed for each sex to enter and find their appropriate notch and for many children to go wild. One pre-schooler threw his plastic truck into the air again and again; depending on the expansive carpet to give the thing a soft landing. AW couldn't easily squeeze into the main group where the high Shaykhs sat at the front close to the implanted *midrab*.

It was Shaykh Efendi who had reopened the mosque after the Greeks were defeated by the Turkish Army in 1974; someone passed on this anecdote to AW. Maulana was given that official role. Now in one of those key recovered structures the nation was again saying goodbye to him and witnessing his profound impact on all their lives. Outside, the high-wall divide between the Turkish and Greek Cyprus was a few blocks away. These streets are nicknamed 'Murderers' Way' because of all the executions of Turkish Cypriots that happened in the city before the war, before the Turkish army invaded. Some in the group historically aware felt how streets wound on but led nowhere except to a boundary established by political powers—the designated Forbidden Zone. That at odds with the generous saint whose motives had been to unify. The night warm; enveloping ancient sculpted arches, domes, doorways and discrete courtyards enhanced the gentle gloom of the tropical darkness forcing everyone to forget the contemporary state of the nations.

Between columns, under archways, around marble ablution features, children outside were going crazy as those inside. The news was out that the city was having a feast, the street kids alert to a chance of free food plundered the proceedings, capturing boxes of bread cakes and sweets, running off into that ancient world with their arms full of sweet deep-fried balls and *halva* slices with dates and almonds. They escaped much notice slipping back to an earlier undivided age if such once existed. The main attendees too busy eating outside or praying inside. Perhaps they all felt the slippage, the lassitude, the freedom to scoff as much as you liked as if each had drifted from modern constraints into another time.

When everyone—mother, father and child—had been fed four times there was still so much left that an officially apparelled woman and a bald-headed black-suited man, balancing large trays, hurried back and forth trying to give away scented colourful sweets and other delicious titbits to satiated worshippers.

In a benched alcove under the gloomy sodium lights a couple exchanged pleasantries—her *hijab* V-shaped down her coated back and his turban-bands and long cloak formed an outline. A tourist viewing point had become a love nook of two muffled voices. Wild youngsters played deregulated football in another connected square.

AW thought how pleased Shaykh Efendi would be to see the hard-faced urchins of the alleys softened by the abundance of goodies that his death provided. AW couldn't help but grieve for the missing statues in the niches around the cathedral-cum-masjid. Their absence urged him to acknowledge history's unknown persons—unnamed who did this and that, accomplished and destroyed, those to whom this edifice was dedicated. If Istanbul was re-invaded, its ornate calligraphy whitewashed the consequence would be the same—he would feel dislocated from people and events; in lost details endure a separation between past and present until all anyone saw were fragments of the mosaic of the human family.

He loved offering his secured seat to an exhausted mother, father and little daughter, not only as an act of charity but as if he was wedged into that human family and it couldn't survive without him or him without them. Was this quaint gesture taking place among thousands, an antidote for the vacant raped niches?

The word had gone around it was time to return to the buses. The gigantic structure threw out its temporary inhabitants. It had had enough of designed practice; it wanted to return to the sacred emptiness and non-division of the faith no one can celebrate.

The *murid*s made their way back through the tangled lanes, enough following enough path-finders that the way became a trampled route; no one ended up lost. All the separated separately burdened and excited individuals and small groups returned to the coaches for the journey back to Lefke. The gears of the bus growled nearing midnight as much as they did in the late afternoon approaching sunset. The city seemed to synchronise its traffic lights to green to assist AW's retreat back to the orange grove spotted valley, to its dancing date palms, its Pir Pasha and *dergāh* back to Shaykh Efendi's realm.

> The day star rises
> through a veil of palms
> my auntie called me
> 'the first ray of sunlight'
> a young *murid* said.

VI

Every night the stars were a spangled display, arranged in strange patterns or placed in an unfamiliar quarter of the sky. Either way AW couldn't easily recognise known constellations. He was in the northern hemisphere; the same galactic picture as at home shone before his eyes but differently conceived. One night past 12 o'clock he grew excited, spotting overhead the Plough and from there began to re-map the accustomed star-patterns that suggested images and stories, but after that strong set of seven astral lights he was quickly lost again in the beauty of otherly ordered forms.

AW stood in the precinct of Pir Osman Pasha's mosque not far from the iron-rod gate that screeched when opened or closed with a sound that felt like more than the chances of fatigue, but as if someone had contrived to replicate that wrenching squeal of metal on metal anytime a visitor approached or departed. To mark a stepping from one space to another the searching eek prepared an incomer for an act of worship or to return to the patient surrounding landscape. Past midnight the screech was more pronounced.

An hour or so earlier the white-turbaned key-holder had left AW to lock the mosque's tall doors. AW had arrived late to pray *isha* and all at once was performing his devotions in isolation in semi-darkness, in contrast to the congregated crushes of other nights and days.

A sole lamp on the left of the *mihrab* hollow tempered the darkness. He aligned his chair with that scooped out space along the southern wall. Those days he couldn't go down in *sajda*; his knees were too stiff. He had to stand then bow but instead of prostrating settled back into a chair and lowered his forehead onto the folded tops of his hands to imitate a descent to the floor. Sometimes AW could feel falling towards the carpet, the repeated action over years had been printed on consciousness and the suggestion of being prostrate half-fulfilled that stage of worship. The three-arched structure was ceilinged with wooden beams supporting varnished planks that gleamed in the lamp light. He had locked the door so no one would haphazardly intrude. The air grew intense with the pressure of other presences: past worshippers who had never completely left, an impression of them remained. It seemed an Ottoman gathering stood around him as if he could half make out high turbans and stately floral robes so much taller than him; they approached then vanished into imagination. The prayer deepened the presence or the infinite to which no particular time-frame could be assigned. His dis-able-ment a gamey knee as his father would have echoed, didn't diminish the potency of prayer.

Through the grilled closed windows in the gloom could be glimpsed the outline of Pir Pasha's tomb. A strange honour to be allowed to practise here alone, no one watching, no one making mistakes except AW, no one going too fast or too slow, counting their beads at a break-neck speed. Everything at the Sufi novice's pace and level of skill, he had to carry the whole performance, but another was present and he guessed Maulana had come along to see how his *murid* was acting. A certain change in air quality, in sensitivity, a feeling of being observed by loving unworldly eyes, an inner vision of a tilt of the brow, a part-formed bearded chin, soft airy bubbles for cheeks.

AW knew it was Maulana. His spirit but more than spirit was roaming to see what his followers were up to, to see if he could inspire them to greater revelation and presence and to a sweeter peace. Now there was no awareness of others congregating around; Shaykh Efendi occupied the space with unfathomable love, that love unstiffened the hard strained white plaster, made AW feel fearless and unchallenged. He had opened a space in which AW's head could lower to the patterned carpet when his physical body had lost that capacity. He shuttered him with humility that squeezed out moisture around living eyes. Now it seemed not only that the Holy One's entire being reached into every corner of the room, but that the mosque was braced up by his presence; he had replaced the stone columns and arches, the plastered walls, the grilled windows. Nothing was necessary except his reality. How could such a being as his wish to visit a weakling like AW? Abdul Wadud pined.

now the key-holder
trusts—what other
doors might spring open

*   *   *

chasing flood water
a scarlet and white toy boat
in the conduit

at the *dergāh*
each drip-catching bucket's
rim over-flowing

A Mulberry tree
in a Sufi's garden—who
can taste love's sweetness

a hooded woman
names perfumes she remembers
from the Shaykh's garden

pre-time prickly pears
what colour are their flowers?
Perfected yellow.

VII

While at his stall, sitting by a white plastic rectangular table with rounded corners, AW became inconspicuous; could observe the many goings-on near the old Shaykh's doorway. This space often was the reserve of visiting women who came and went, shoes clacking and dresses swishing. Families came and went, children pulling make-believe luggage or leaning from strollers or prams. The fathers meeting the wife and children; the husband would have walked from the nearby *dergāh* and the other two from inside the Shaykh's house. Beside AW's table a stone wall projected partially rendered in which some symbols had been furtively etched, a pentangle being one. The pattern of stone blocks suggested a pier for an archway which had long been removed perhaps to benefit the traffic along the narrow road.

Under the vanished keystone and curved supports, many visitors that had arrived within the last few days to join in the commemoration of Maulana prepared to leave, often picked up in one of a bevy of cars and mini-cabs and Land Rovers. Suitcases would be stowed in the boot and the *hijab*ed and prayer-hatted with their sometimes covered daughters would plunge into the passenger seats. Arrivers and Departers seemed privileged under and around the dismembered portico on the right side of the double-door entrance. While engines purred or chuddered, red, grey, black, white or brown vehicles waited their human haulage.

With each national distinction in some character trait or in their apparel, the soon-to-depart would receive last-minute gifts: fruit from the Shaykh's garden, oranges and lemons, but also baking delicacies, or gifts of scarves, pictures of Maulana or emblems. AW guessed their family bonds with the Shaykh which allowed them to stay in the big house with double blue doors. Men were discouraged from hanging around the entrance but in the medley of a large number of *murid*s, often men, women and children conversed and occupied this segregated space.

Sometimes their attention was directed toward AW's stall which led to only the odd sale because most of those coming and going were not English, more likely Turkish or German. Hugs and kisses were beyond words, male and female signs of feelings—regret at departures, joy in the expectation of seeing them again or satisfaction that every travel connection had gone to plan, intricate itineraries had been realised. Leaving, when fulfilling their tactics, was more tolerable, yet required an elemental action to signal the fruition of a visit.

Despite its sparseness water was used to honour regretted departures. Suddenly from the Shaykh's house across the threshold a resident of the family came running with a big glass jug brimming with clear water. Then as the vehicle started to purr away, flung the jug's content against the back window of minibuses or saloons or estates or hatchbacks, against five doors, two doors or four. The liquid showered the car, whose occupants turned with feint surprise. They smiled to see the emotions on the resident's face of wishing-washing goodbye with the intention that this soaking would speed the others on their passage and also suggested their probable return to the same site where a second dousing would be waiting. The perishable liquid sparkled and slid off the slanted tails of blue, green, whites, blacks and many other colours, as many as the flower hues in the Shaykh's garden.

This gesture was supported by the island mentality—those surrounded by seas knew the departing in almost all cases would be venturing over waves by ferry or plane—the exponent of this ritual hoped the sea would be kind to its travellers. The silent action, except for the pronounced splash, seemed to say 'May the sea be kind to you, may the Shaykh's mercy oceans be with you, may Allah ﷻ be with you.'

AW marvelled at this capacious way of parting; where water was so precious, another 'twinkling horse', but not more valuable than saying to the dear ones driving off that they were also precious. The sadness had been displaced by excitement; an unpredictable condition had entered the consequent mood of departure. This flight of water, in a half-measurable arc: how would it fall, would it reach its target—would the purposeful thrower succeed to land the fluid on the right location? This hinted a bow to fate, like when one attempts to blow out every candle on a birthday cake with one sucked-in puff. The water ceremony was reserved for the females as if the task of ensuring a journey, arrival and return had to be in their soft hands. It was given to someone from the kitchen, an underling, who'd cut through ranks of kissing, hugging and bowing to fling their emotions, to slosh all our feelings on the back of a disappearing car.

> Did we hit or not
> a small black snake
> crossing the road
> on that first hot day
> in Northern Cyprus?
>
> When I arrived
> she started to tell me
> about her love of snakes—
> the poisonous one
> with the powerful head
> a triangular design
> fangs that dug in
> and clung on.
>
> 'And it's deaf'
> she said, 'you can step
> on it—so can't hear your
> approach—it strikes
> without a warning.'

VIII

Fasting on the seventh day making *wudu* at Pir Osman Pasha, AW prayed in semi-darkness outside the mosque. Then along came in the early morning the water-freer. After each downpour he arrived on a rickety motorcycle with his eccentric implements to unblock the small concrete canals that fed the often thirsty and parched island.

So many thoughts plunged through AW's mind and heart. He had to go off and start walking among the hills around Lefke up the citrus-fruited valleys towards sandpaper slopes now freckled with green from surprise deluges of recent days.

Perhaps we should leave Abdul Wadud there with shoes a little too worn and his little-known dreams, his brown satchel curved against his side and his faded prayer hat on his balding head. Now and then he might limp from that stiff left knee that's endured much kneeling on prayer mats and been tested on long, long treks. His shadow stretches ahead down the road by the gouged-out abandoned mine exposing the layers of inner rock on a mountain side as he walks towards but not into the Forbidden Zone. He questions: do we all have a forbidden zone? He might greet someone he knows or half-knows or doesn't know with *salaams*, his *tasbīh* twirling through his fingers, AW doing *salawāt* or chanting inwardly and sometimes aloud one or other of the beautiful names of Allah, *Ya Wadud* for an example, the Loving One.

It's all about that emotion being transcended to become that emotion refined into a more complete way of behaving—that without fail extended goodness towards his companion human beings and restrained temptations to impose an evil thought or action. Abdul Wadud understood he would be asking for forgiveness until and beyond the last day of his life. He could as well as submit to be rebellious; an angelic rapscallion if such can exist. For now he would recognise his enfeebled moral and physical state by plying his *tasbīh*, round and round the beads would trickle through his fingers like sacred water being offered to Maulana, may Allah ﷻ bless his soul. Perhaps we should leave him as he slips away from Lefke and the *dergāh* past twilight, *adhān* for *isha* sounding through the hills, no shadow as yet from the moon between sporadic street lamps.

IX

AW on one foot-sojourn met a grey figure, stooped with age and smiling, standing on the roadside. The older man was dressed in clothes AW couldn't relate to. None of the brothers wore this style of garment or sisters or anyone back home or further back in his childhood home across the ocean. The apparition that was flesh and bone stood at peace with the new day's gaining darkness and chill in the young night, in no hurry to disappear anywhere, all earthly duties in abeyance. AW greeted him with *salaams* as was the novice's custom. The grey figure handed Abdul Wadud a torn off piece of white paper—it read in AW's language—you'll die at this road's end. AW smiled when perhaps he should have been horrified. He replied—this is the road of life and its conclusion is death. But he added with an intake of breath and shake of thoughts, his prayer hat askew that he hoped to die before that ending, he hoped to die before he died. The spectral mortal lifted his head and revealed the expression of intense pleasure with cheeks bulging, his eyes sparkling and his white beard a tangle of radiance.

We can't imagine what's beyond death of the ego, how mountains and valleys might sound and look, what shades paint twilight and dawn when we see through eyes with rusted scales removed. How will we kiss with untarnished lips, can we picture that softness, what will we feel when one freed human being meets another on the road at twilight? May Allah grant us His pleasure, peace and His love. May He forgive His creation and bless the centuries to come.

Glossary

Adhān: The Islamic call to prayer, recited at prescribed times of the day.

Armageddon: According to the *Book of Revelation*, the site of a battle during the end of times.

Asr: An afternoon prayer, the third offered by Muslims daily.

As-salām alaykum: An Arabic greeting often used by Muslims around the world, meaning 'Peace be with you'.

Asmah Plaj: in North Cyprus, famous for its ancient grapevine.

Beshparmak: The Pentadactylos, the Five-Finger Mountains in North Cyprus.

Dergāh: Sufi lodge, where the Shaykh meets his *murids*, where obligatory prayers and *dhikr* are performed, where talks are given.

Dhikr: Ritual chanting and music to remember Allah ﷻ. The word literally means 'remembrance' or 'invocation'.

Dolmush: Long local taxi, usually black.

Du'a: An invocation, an act of supplication, profound worship.

Efendi: An Ottoman/Turkish title of respect, meaning 'Sir'.

Fajr: The dawn prayer, practised by Muslims before the sun rises.

Forbidden Zone: Neutral or buffer zone between Greek and Turkish Cypriots established after 1974.

Hajj: An annual pilgrimage to Mecca, a mandatory religious duty for Muslims, to be carried out at least once in their lifetime.

Halva: A Middle Eastern sweet made of sesame flour and honey.

Hijab: In common usage, refers to the headscarf worn by Muslim women.

Imam: A leader of the prayers or Muslim community.

Isha: The evening prayer, approximately two hours after sunset, the fifth daily prayer performed by Muslims.

Jinn: Unseen creatures in Islamic belief as well as in pre-Islamic Arabian mythology, created from fire.

Jubba: A long outer garment commonly worn by Muslim men and women, especially in Arab countries.

Jum'a: A congregational prayer that Muslims hold every Friday just after noon, in the place of *zuhr*, the midday prayer.

Ka'aba: A cuboid building at the centre of Islam's most sacred mosque, Al-Masjid al-Haram, in Mecca, Saudi Arabia.

Lahmacun: Turkish pizza.

Lefke: Small town in North Cyprus where Shaykh Efendi lived.

Maghrib: The dusk prayer, practised by Muslim after the sun sets.

Majnun: An archetypal name for someone acting insane, derived from the Persian love story *Layla and Majnun*, by Nizami. To a Sufi it represents the unqualified love for Allah ﷻ a *murid* may achieve.

Maqam: A 'station', a sacred site, where a saint is buried, for example.

Mawlid: The observance of the birthday of the Islamic prophet Muhammad ﷺ; a generic term for birthday celebrations of other historical religious figures such as Sufi saints.

Maulana: Arabic meaning 'our master'.

Mihrab: A semi-circular niche in the wall of a mosque indicating the direction to Mecca, the direction that Muslims face when praying.

Murid: 'Committed one', refers to a follower of a Shaykh.

Naqsh: Suggests the love of Allah ﷻ is stamped on a Sufi's or follower's heart. Omar Khayyam writes, 'Humankind, The circle of this is like a ring/There is no doubt at all that we are the/Naqsh, the Design of its bezel.' The term indicates one who engages in such practice that their devotion makes a mark, stamp, design on the heart. Thus, Shaykh Efendi was a Naqshbandi shaykh.

Nūr: Light, or Divine Light.

Oudh: Incense, derived from the wood of the tropical Agar tree.

Qutub Osman: Ottoman saint whose tomb is in North Cyprus.

Rakat: Prescribed movements and words followed by Muslims while offering prayers to Allah ﷻ.

Sajjada: Prayer mats.

Sajda: Prostration during prayer; when on his knees the worshipper places his forehead on the ground, submitting to Allah ﷻ.

Salawāt: Salutations reserved for the Prophet Muhammad ﷺ.

Salāt: Formal prayers in Islam practised five times a day.

Sayyidi: Master.

Shahada: A creed declaring belief in the oneness of God and Muhammad ﷺ as His Prophet and Messenger. Would-be Muslims recite *shahada* at their entry into the faith and Islamic community.

Shaitan: The devil.

Shāhid: Witness.

Shahīd: Martyr.

Shaykh: Teacher, wise one, revered master, enlightened man.

Sufi: *Tasawwuf* is an Islamic concept denoting the inner, mystical dimension of Islam. A Sufi is a practitioner of the tradition of *tasawwuf.*

Sunnah prayer: Arabic for 'usual practice' referring to the way of life prescribed for Muslims based on the teachings and practices of the Prophet Muhammad ﷺ and interpretations of the Qur'an.

Tasbīh: Prayer beads, used for *dhikr.*

Tor: A rock formation.

Vouni: Greek for 'mountain'; an excavation site 9 km to the west of Lefke dating to around the 5th century BC. The site of a palace and surrounding township, probably built during the period of Persian occupation and domination, expanded by successive rulers, and destroyed by fire and the inhabitants of nearby Soli. A temple of Athena also perches on the hillside.

The Warrior: Constellation Orion, in Arabic, the Great Hunter.

Wadi: A valley or a riverbed.

Waraqa: A Christian Ebionite priest, one of the first to believe in the prophecy of Muhammad ﷺ; he was the paternal cousin of Muhammad's wife, Khadijah.

Wudu: The Islamic procedure for washing parts of the body using water, typically in preparation for formal prayers.

Ya Sīn: A chapter of the Qur'an, recited as a prayer for the dead, especially martyrs, saints; used at other times such as in *fajr* prayer. *Ya Sīn* is the core or heart of the Qur'an.

Ziyāra: (Turkish rendering *ziyaret*) An Arabic term meaning 'visit' referring to a pilgrimage to sites associated with Muhammad ﷺ, his family members and descendants, his companions and other venerated figures in Islam, such as prophets, Sufi saints and Islamic scholars.

Zuhr: The midday prayer, the second daily prayer performed by Muslims.